MW00609239

A GIFT FOR

_____

FROM

_____

DATE

_____

THE WHOLE STORY

A 52-WEEK DEVOTIONAL JOURNEY
THROUGH EVERY BOOK *of* THE BIBLE

DR. DAVID JEREMIAH

THOMAS NELSON
Since 1798

The Bible is forever. It will never change. It will never fail. It will never let you down. It cannot ever be out of date. You can count on it to be there for you when you need it. It endures forever.

—DAVID JEREMIAH

CONTENTS

INTRODUCTION

THE BIBLE IS FOREVER

THROUGHOUT MY YEARS OF TEACHING and ministry, my deepest desire has been for more people to know what the Bible says, what it means, and what it means for their life. Considering the events of the past few years, studying God's Word has never been more critical. It is the only place we can turn to for absolute truth. By understanding the depths of God's love and the extent of His power, we can find an anchor for our soul and hope for tomorrow.

Lining our bookshelves with dozens of Bible translations is not enough. Turning the tide in our world starts with turning the pages of Scripture.

After more than forty years of preaching and teaching God's Word, I am still discovering new insights and applications within its pages. And I have no doubt you will find the

> *The Bible is the only place we can turn to for absolute truth.*

1

same. So let me reintroduce you to the Book that offers wisdom, insight, and instruction for each new day.

As we journey through *The Whole Story*, I pray that the Bible will fill your memory, rule your heart, and guide your feet. Welcome to the adventure!

A SUPERNATURAL BOOK

The Bible was written in three languages over a span of fifteen hundred years by approximately forty human authors from all walks of life. Hailing from the Middle East, Mesopotamia, Asia Minor, and Southern Europe, these men were kings, farmers, historians, fishermen, prophets, apostles, free men, and slaves. For all their differences, they shared a distinctive connection: the Spirit of God guided them so that the words they recorded were nothing less than the very words of God.

There is simply no other explanation for the Bible's accuracy and coherency. Dr. Henry Morris wrote, "The individual writers, at the time of writing, had no idea that their message was eventually to be incorporated into such a Book, but each nevertheless fits perfectly into place and serves its own unique purpose as a component of the whole. Anyone who diligently studies the Bible will continually find remarkable structural and mathematical patterns woven throughout its fabric, with an intricacy and symmetry incapable of explanation by chance or collusion."[1]

Throughout the ages, God's eternal Word has withstood countless campaigns to silence it. In AD 303, Rome's emperor, Diocletian, ordered the burning of Bibles and the martyrdom of Christians. Twenty years later, a new emperor, Constantine, proclaimed the Bible to be the infallible judge of all truth. In the eighteenth century, the French philosopher Voltaire predicted that God's Word would lose its voice within fifty years. Half a century later, eyewitness accounts suggest that the Geneva Bible Society was printing Bibles in Voltaire's former house on his very own printing presses. Today, the Bible is difficult to obtain or even illegal in fifty-two countries, but in keeping with history, each new wave of persecution spreads the gospel farther.[2]

> *Throughout the ages, God's eternal Word has withstood countless campaigns to silence it.*

Each time someone sounds the Bible's death knell, it rises from the ashes. Moses has outlived Voltaire. Isaiah has outlasted Ingersoll. The apostles have outsmarted the agnostics. And the prophets have overpowered the professors. In the words of Isaiah, "The grass withers, the flower fades, but the word of our God stands forever" (40:8).

A PERFECT BOOK

The Bible has always been a difference maker. Over the years, I have watched this Book and the Savior it represents permanently change people's lives. But do not take my word for it—Scripture has plenty to say for itself. Consider Psalm 19:7–11:

> The law of the LORD is perfect, converting the soul;
> The testimony of the LORD is sure, making wise the simple;

The statutes of the LORD are right, rejoicing the heart;
The commandment of the LORD is pure, enlightening
    the eyes;
The fear of the LORD is clean, enduring forever;
The judgments of the LORD are true and righteous altogether.
More to be desired are they than gold,
Yea, than much fine gold;
Sweeter also than honey and the honeycomb.
Moreover by them Your servant is warned,
And in keeping them there is great reward.

This psalm, written by David, combines some of the most splendid Hebrew poetry with some of the most excellent theology you will find in one place. It is a picture of parallel structure, symbolism, and poetry. At the same time, it gives us great insight into the power and influence of God's Word.

Let's peel back the poetry for a moment and examine the grammar. This passage lists six different names or synonyms for the Bible: "the law . . . the testimony . . . the statutes . . . the commandment . . . the fear . . . the judgments." Any one of these could replace "Bible" in a sentence, but they provide additional information about its Author and its purpose. All six of them make clear that the Bible is "of the Lord." Scripture comes directly from Him. They also tell us that this is not a book to read and put back on the shelf. The Bible is a book for us to obey.

Be transformed by the renewing of your mind.
ROMANS 12:2

In this passage, David gives seven adjectives to describe the Bible. He calls God's Word "perfect . . . sure . . . right . . . pure . . . clean . . . true . . . [and] righteous." All those lengthy genealogies? Perfect. The end-times prophecies? Surer than death and taxes. The commandments? Right and true. God's judgment? Righteous and pure. From cover to cover, the Bible is all these things.

A POWERFUL BOOK

Once we understand the authority and perfection of God's Word, we can unleash its power to transform our lives.

THE BIBLE WILL RESTORE OUR SOULS. Earlier in Psalm 19, David explained how God's creation reveals who He is, but it is the Word that teaches us how to respond to God. Romans 10:17 says, "Faith comes by hearing, and hearing by the word of God." The Bible is uniquely able to bring people to salvation.

THE BIBLE WILL RENEW OUR MINDS. Whether we are looking for relationship advice, business principles, or money management, it's all in the pages of the Bible. Scripture also gives us a way to withstand the secular, often perverse influence of our world. As Christians, we can choose to "be transformed by the renewing of [our] mind" instead of conforming to the world (Romans 12:2).

THE BIBLE WILL REJOICE OUR HEARTS. We all know people who spend their lives searching for happiness in the wrong places. Whether they look to their careers, relationships, or finances, they always come up empty. Those things cannot provide true satisfaction, but God's Word can and does. Even Jeremiah, who was known as "the weeping prophet," managed to find joy in its pages. Jeremiah 15:16 says, "When I discovered your words, I devoured them. They are my joy and my heart's delight, for I bear your name, O LORD God of Heaven's Armies" (NLT). That's what God's Word will do for you and me. It will restore our souls, renew our minds, and rejoice our hearts.

THE BIBLE WILL REFOCUS OUR VISION. Anyone who has visited an optometrist has experience with a phoropter. It is the machine that clicks through different lenses to determine which one provides the most optimal vision. In the process, some lenses improve our sight while others make it fuzzier. Spiritually speaking, we need to ask ourselves if we perceive things as they truly are. When we view the world through our prejudices, experiences, or background, we look through the wrong lens. But with the Bible as our lens, we can discern the reality about ourselves and the world around us.

THE BIBLE WILL REFRESH OUR LIVES. It's hard to understand unless you have experienced it, but the Bible is a cleansing agent. Studying God's Word shows us our impurities and helps us get rid of them. It will wash our hearts and renew us. In the words of Psalm 119:9, "How can a young man cleanse his way? By taking heed according to Your word."

THE BIBLE WILL REPLACE OUR DOUBTS. There are very few certainties in this life. But every word in God's Book is true—all of it, from the beginning to the end. Psalm 18:30 proclaims, "As for God, His way is perfect; the word of the LORD is proven; He is a shield to all who trust in Him." Throughout history, many brilliant minds have tried to destroy the Bible, and they have all failed. In fact, several ended up becoming followers of Christ because they could not deny the evidence for the Bible's historicity and inspiration. Some books are worth doubting, but the Bible is not one of them.

THE BIBLE WILL REORDER OUR VALUES. We can determine a lot about our priorities by the way we spend our time, money, and effort. C.S. Lewis wrote, "Aim at Heaven and you will get Earth 'thrown in': aim at Earth and you will get neither."[3] We need to ask ourselves where we are aiming. In Matthew 6:33, Jesus described our priorities this way: "Seek first the kingdom of God and His righteousness, and all these things shall be added to you."

THE BIBLE WILL REDIRECT OUR PATHS. Not too many people enjoy hearing the word "no," but Scripture's warnings will often keep us from experiencing painful disasters if we will heed them. People have told me, "Well, Pastor, sometimes it's easier to receive God's forgiveness than His permission." Don't do that. When the Bible tells you not to do something, it is a warning for your protection. Proverbs 12:15 says, "The way of a fool is right in his own eyes, but he who heeds counsel is wise." We cannot see the consequences of our choices the way God can. Listen to the One who knows the end from the beginning.

THE BIBLE WILL REWARD OUR OBEDIENCE. Of all the people I know, the happiest are those who know Jesus Christ and have committed to following Him wherever He takes them. They understand that God's Word is their source of instruction for life. James 1:25 tells us, "But he who looks into the perfect law of liberty and continues in it, and is not a forgetful hearer but a doer of the work, this one will be blessed in what he does."

Nothing in life is more important than understanding the Bible. It draws us into a closer relationship with the Lord and positions us to receive His blessings. My prayer is that *The Whole Story* will encourage you to make the study of God's Word a priority in your life. In the words of Peter, "May God give you more and more grace and peace as you grow in your knowledge of God and Jesus our Lord" (2 Peter 1:2 NLT).

A PERSONAL BOOK

The challenges of living an authentic Christian life call for more than an initial experience with God. We need His wisdom every day. Colossians 1:9 records Paul's prayer for the church of Colossae, a prayer that makes a valuable distinction. He prayed that the Colossians will be "filled with the knowledge of His will in all wisdom and spiritual understanding." As we study God's Word, we receive wisdom. But Paul reminded us that there is more to our faith than wisdom; we also need to gain spiritual understanding by probing Scripture's instructions consistently. How do we maximize our reception of the Bible's instruction?

PREPARATION. Before reading, select a quiet location and take the time to pray. Ask God to remove all the distractions that could detract from your time with Him.

EXAMINATION. With a pen, pencil, or highlighter in hand, actively read each verse of your chosen passage. Do not be overly concerned with the length of the passage you are studying. Your goal is to gain instruction from the Word, not to scan large amounts of information.

APPLICATION. Transformation occurs one step at a time. Identify one concept you can apply to your life. Ask God how He wants to change you right now in your present circumstances and always.

MEDITATION. Search God's Word, reading and rereading what God has said about those things that need to change in your life. As you apply this new concept to your life, note the changes that need to occur in your attitude, outlook, and conduct.

If you are looking for a respite from this world and hope for the future, you only need to look in your Bible.

MEMORIZATION. Transcribe a particularly impactful part of your Scripture reading onto a note card or in an app on your smartphone. Make it your goal to memorize that portion of your study.

DEMONSTRATION. Translate your study from words into actions. Find one person who needs the encouragement you have received from the passage, and share it with them.

If you are looking for a respite from this world and hope for the future, you only need to look in your Bible. Its pages glow with grace and provide hope and meaning for all who will heed it. Books that Christians often flip past, such as Numbers and Lamentations, are just as "profitable" as well-worn favorites (2 Timothy 3:16). I hope you will enjoy reaching beyond familiar stories as you immerse yourself in the whole counsel of God's Word.

THE OLD TESTAMENT

—⟨∽⟩—

Your iniquities have separated you from your God.

ISAIAH 59:2

THE PENTATEUCH

❦

GENESIS, EXODUS, LEVITICUS, NUMBERS, AND DEUTERONOMY

❦

THE FIRST FIVE BOOKS OF THE OLD TESTAMENT are known as the Pentateuch, or the Torah. From creation to Israel's arrival at the promised land, these books help us understand how sin separated us from God and how quickly the effects of sin spread throughout the world. But these are not just a collection of stories illustrating Israel's sin; they prepare us to know Jesus and point to His grace.

HOPE: A GIFT FROM GOD

GENESIS 1–11

*"I will put enmity between you and the woman, and between your seed and
her Seed; He shall bruise your head, and you shall bruise His heel."*

GENESIS 3:15

MANY WHO ARE NOT FAMILIAR with biblical proph-
ecy wonder if humanity is teetering on the brink of extinction.
Between rogue nations, natural disasters, environmental pollution,
and world powers standing on the edge of insolvency, the future
doesn't look bright.

What wouldn't the average person give for a book that describes
the future of the world and the human race! But such a Book does
exist—God's Holy Word. Starting from creation, it chronicles the
history of the world. And looking forward, the Bible calms our
fears with assurance for the future.

There was a time, in the beginning, when there were no promises of God, fulfilled or unfulfilled. The future of humankind
stretched forth like a blank canvas. And then God spoke the first

prophecy—directly related to man's fall from grace in the garden of Eden. Addressing the serpent that deceived Adam and Eve, God prophesied his ultimate demise.

God gave hope to the first humans by promising that the Seed of Eve, Jesus Christ, would one day crush Satan's head. By the time the apostle Paul wrote to the Roman church, Christ's resurrection from the dead had partially fulfilled that prophecy. But Satan's ultimate demise is still coming: "And the God of peace will crush Satan under your feet shortly" (Romans 16:20).

Dr. Hugh Ross of Reasons to Believe, a science-faith think tank, estimates that the Bible contains "2,500 prophecies . . . about 2,000 of which already have been fulfilled to the letter—no errors."[4] The remaining five hundred or so are yet to be fulfilled. By looking back at fulfilled prophecies, we can have tremendous confidence in the Bible's remaining prophecies.

A VERSE TO WRITE

*"I will establish My covenant with you; and you shall go into the ark—
you, your sons, your wife, and your sons' wives with you."*

GENESIS 6:18

_____

_____

_____

_____

_____

REFLECT ON THIS

Read Genesis 6:5. What was the extent of man's wickedness before the flood?

_____

_____

_____

Read Genesis 6 and Hebrews 11:7. When Noah built the ark in Genesis 6, he did not have a written Bible or thousands of fulfilled prophecies. What reasons do you find for his faithful obedience?

_____

_____

_____

Noah's family survived the flood because Noah obeyed God and believed in His prophecy. The Bible warns that a fiery judgment is coming (Luke 12:49; 2 Peter 3:10). How have you prepared for that day? Who will enter the ark of God's salvation because of your faithful witness?

_____

_____

_____

RECEIVING GOD'S BLESSINGS

GENESIS 12–50

*"I will establish My covenant between Me and you and your descendants
after you in their generations, for an everlasting covenant."*

GENESIS 17:7

WHEN FACED WITH A CHOICE, we naturally select the most desirable option. Football teams draft the most promising young players. Colleges grant scholarships to students who excel academically. Single people spend time with those they find the most compatible.

Not so with God. He selected a childless couple with pagan names to be the ancestors of His chosen people. Nothing about Abram and Sarai's pedigree qualified them for the honor, and there was nothing they could do to deserve God's favor. The only asset they brought to the table was their obedience. And as we know from Scripture, even that was imperfect at best.

The Abrahamic covenant was and is entirely dependent upon God. When it was made, God alone passed through the fire because He was the only One who could fulfill its terms (Genesis 15). Also, there was no provision made for the covenant to be broken or annulled. It permanently established God's unilateral, unconditional commitment to His people.

What does this mean for us today? We, too, are beneficiaries of God's unwavering commitment. God told Abram, "In you all the families of the earth shall be blessed" (Genesis 12:3). We receive this blessing through the Bible and the Messiah. Abram's descendants wrote every book of the Bible except Luke and Acts. Saving grace flowed through Abraham, through the Jewish people, and it has reached us. Praise God for His promise to Israel!

A VERSE TO WRITE

"I will make you a great nation; I will bless you and make your name great; and you shall be a blessing."
GENESIS 12:2

_____

_____

_____

_____

_____

REFLECT ON THIS

God's covenant with Abram extended beyond spiritual blessings. Looking at Genesis 12:1–3 and 17:1–22, what other blessings does the Bible describe?

_____

_____

_____

Read Deuteronomy 7:6–8. What words describe God's feelings for Israel? What reasons do you find for His love?

_____

_____

Read 1 Corinthians 1:26–28. Why does God often call people who are not the most qualified?

_____

_____

_____

In what ways is God calling you to serve Him beyond your qualifications? How will you respond to His call?

_____

_____

GOD LOVES HIS PEOPLE

EXODUS

———— ∾ ————

God heard their groaning, and God remembered His covenant
with Abraham, with Isaac, and with Jacob.

EXODUS 2:24

IN THE BOOK OF EXODUS, we encounter a strange turn
of events. A foreign power enslaved the people with whom God
made an everlasting covenant. Did He forget His covenant? Was
He unable to protect Israel?

Genesis 38 holds the key that unlocks the events of Exodus.
After Judah convinced his brothers to sell Joseph into slavery, he left
home, went to a foreign country, and married a pagan Canaanite
woman. He was only three generations removed from God's covenant, yet his lifestyle was indistinguishable from the wicked culture
of his day.

Judah's life is but one example of the Canaanites' corrupting
influence on Israel. Every time the Hebrews got mixed up with the
Canaanites, sin and corruption followed. Joseph's time in Egypt

allowed God to prepare a protected place for His people to be free from society's evil influence.

After 430 years in Egypt, the Israelites numbered more than two million people. They had maintained their distinct identity, and they were ready to journey to the promised land. So God provided a leader to guide them out of bondage and instructions for holy living.

Many people think of the Ten Commandments as an outdated list of dos and don'ts. But the commandments are best viewed as Almighty God's principles for successful living. It would have been unloving for God to turn His people loose among evil influences without giving them the tools to thrive.

A VERSE TO WRITE

Then Moses and the children of Israel sang this song to the LORD,
and spoke, saying: "I will sing to the LORD, for He has triumphed
gloriously! The horse and its rider He has thrown into the sea!"

EXODUS 15:1

_____

_____

_____

_____

_____

_____

REFLECT ON THIS

After the golden calf incident and the destruction of the first set of stone tablets, Moses met with God to receive a second set. How does God describe Himself at this meeting? (Exodus 34:6–7)

_____

_____

_____

The first three commandments teach us how to revere and worship the Lord (Exodus 20:1–7). Why would God place such an emphasis on worship? Support your answer with Scripture.

_____

_____

_____

_____

Not all idols are made from wood and stone. Anything that interferes with your worship of Almighty God constitutes an idol. It could be a relationship, a goal, or a hobby. How has idolatry seeped into your life? How will you recommit your affections to the Lord?

_____

_____

_____

_____

BE LIFTED UP

LEVITICUS AND NUMBERS

Then the Lord said to Moses, "Make a fiery serpent, and set it on a pole; and it shall be that everyone who is bitten, when he looks at it, shall live."

NUMBERS 21:8

PREACHERS STAND ON PLATFORMS; flags are raised to the top of poles; signs are put high up on billboards. Raising something high makes it visible to more people and gives it a sense of importance. That's why God told Moses to make a serpent out of bronze, set it on a pole, and raise it up so the Israelites could see it. God had punished their sin by allowing serpents into their camp, and Moses' bronze serpent became a source of deliverance for them when they gazed on it and believed (Numbers 21:4–9).

Knowing that the Jews would grasp the metaphor immediately, Jesus said that He would be "lifted up" and become a source of salvation to all who looked to Him (John 3:14–15; 12:32). By "lifted up," He was referring to the Roman cross that lay ahead of Him. His words were prophetic—His death on a cross has drawn millions to Him for two thousand years. We continue to lift Him up today in the Lord's Supper, "[proclaiming] the Lord's death till

He comes" (1 Corinthians 11:26). We also lift Him up as we praise Him for His blessings in our lives.

Knowing the Old Testament informs what we read in the New Testament. We, like those in the early church, can make connections to promises God made centuries ago. We have a depth of understanding that goes beyond the words on the page and extends to the meaning certain words and stories bring. Those layers of meaning not only point us to Jesus but also build our faith and compound our blessing for the world to see.

Our lives should continually point the world to Jesus Christ— lifting Him up for all to see and be saved.

A VERSE TO WRITE

Moses made a bronze serpent, and put it on a pole; and so it was, if a serpent had bitten anyone, when he looked at the bronze serpent, he lived.

NUMBERS 21:9

_____

_____

_____

_____

_____

REFLECT ON THIS

How do you "lift up" Christ in your daily life?

_____

_____

_____

_____

Read Leviticus 16:21–22. How did the goat that was freed into the wilderness redeem the sins of the children of Israel? How does this foreshadow Christ's redemption of our sins?

_____

_____

_____

_____

OUR LOVE FOR GOD AND OTHERS

DEUTERONOMY

*Hear, O Israel: The L*ORD *our God, the L*ORD *is one! You shall love the L*ORD
your God with all your heart, with all your soul, and with all your strength.

DEUTERONOMY 6:4–5

AFTER FLEEING EGYPT, THE CHILDREN of Israel spent forty years wandering in the Sinai wilderness. They were free from oppression, but they needed to learn how to live before a holy God. The Lord required more than empty words about their affection for Him—He demanded their obedience.

Nearing the end of his life, Moses gave a series of speeches to remind Israel of God's commandments. Many of these are recorded in the book of Deuteronomy. Today's passage is known as the *Shema* because this is the Hebrew word for "hear." As the nation entered Canaan, a land filled with many gods, the *Shema* affirmed the nature of the one true God.

When Jesus was asked about the greatest commandment, He answered by giving two. To the *Shema*, He added the command to "love your neighbor as yourself" (Matthew 22:39). Isn't that an excellent summary of the Ten Commandments? The first four teach us how to live out our love for God, and the remaining commandments teach us what it means to love other people. First John 4:20 says, "If someone says, 'I love God,' and hates his brother, he is a liar; for he who does not love his brother whom he has seen, how can he love God whom he has not seen?"

> *I believe the Bible is the best gift God has ever given to man. All the good from the Savior of the world is communicated to us through this Book.*
> **ABRAHAM LINCOLN**

In the *Shema*, there are three aspects of our love for God: heart, soul, and strength. When Jesus cites it in the Gospels, He adds "mind" to the list. Our love for God is to be all-encompassing. Our thoughts, decisions, desires, everything within us, and all the resources at our disposal are instruments we can use to demonstrate our love for God. This ancient prayer reminds us that true faith is rooted in our dynamic, loving, mindful relationship with the Lord our God.

A VERSE TO WRITE

The Lord, He is the One who goes before you. He will be with you, He will not leave you nor forsake you; do not fear nor be dismayed.
DEUTERONOMY 31:8

REFLECT ON THIS

The Bible's definition of *love* is different from the popular idea of it being an emotional feeling. How do the following verses describe love? Deuteronomy 10:12; 11:1, 13, 22; 19:9; 30:16; John 14:15; 15:12–14.

_____

_____

_____

Why should we love God? See Psalm 86:15; Romans 5:8; Galatians 2:20; Ephesians 2:4–5; 1 John 3:1; 4:19.

_____

_____

_____

We all know people who are more challenging to love than others. How will you commit to demonstrating the love of Christ in those relationships?

_____

_____

_____

THE TRUTH IS THIS: GOD IS SAYING, "I WANT YOU TO KNOW RIGHT NOW THAT ALL OF HISTORY, INCLUDING THE PORTION CONSTITUTING YOUR LIFE, IS COMPLETELY UNDER MY CONTROL. NO MATTER HOW THINGS MAY APPEAR, EVERY LITTLE DETAIL IS PART OF A VERY BEAUTIFUL PICTURE. BUT I'M LEAVING THOSE DETAILS AS CHALLENGES OF FAITH TO PREPARE YOU FOR THE WORLD WE WILL SHARE ONE DAY. YOU MUST TRUST ME IN THOSE SMALLER THINGS, KNOWING THAT THE LARGER THINGS ARE ALL ESTABLISHED."[5]

DAVID JEREMIAH

THE HISTORICAL BOOKS

JOSHUA, JUDGES, RUTH, 1 AND
2 SAMUEL, 1 AND 2 KINGS, 1
AND 2 CHRONICLES, EZRA,
NEHEMIAH, AND ESTHER

JOSHUA MARKS THE BEGINNING of twelve historical
books, which chronicle pivotal events in Israel's history as a nation,
including Israel's entry into the promised land, the monarchy, the
destruction of Israel by Assyria and Babylon, and the Jews' return
from exile in Babylon.

GOD KEEPS HIS PROMISES

JOSHUA

⁓

*Joshua said to the people, "Sanctify yourselves, for tomorrow
the LORD will do wonders among you."*

JOSHUA 3:5

EVERY ISRAELITE, EXCEPT JOSHUA AND CALEB, who
could remember life in Egypt had passed away, including Moses. The
current generation of Israelites was poised to enter the promised land.
Still, they faced challenges they had only heard about from their
fathers—giants, fortified cities, and military forces with cutting-edge
iron armory. Behind them lay the wilderness and the graves of their
disobedient parents. Before them stretched the abundance of the
promised land. How did this young nation face an unknown future?

REFLECTION. Everything about Israel's wilderness wandering was miraculous. One army general calculated that it would
have taken fifteen hundred to four thousand tons of food a day
to sustain so many people. With no lakes or oceans around, they
also needed eleven million gallons of water each day. When they

pitched camp, they required an area one-third the size of Rhode Island. Despite these odds, the people of Israel never went hungry, and their clothes and shoes didn't wear out for four decades. Remembering how God had provided in the past was the key to facing their future.

FOCUS. Symbolic of God's presence, the ark of the covenant was carried on the shoulders of the priests, far ahead of the community. Why? God wanted every man, woman, and child to fix their gaze on Him. Focus is a matter of perspective. By seeing Him in the midst of their situation, God's people could move forward without fear.

BELIEF. It's one thing to know about a promise. It's another matter to act on that promise. The priests carrying the ark of the covenant had to believe that God would provide a way for them to cross the Jordan. With 3.5 million people watching, they placed their feet in the Jordan's floodwaters *before* God pulled back the water (Joshua 3:15).

The Israelites stepped into the promised land because they recognized God's past provision, His presence, and His promises for their future.

A VERSE TO WRITE

"Be strong and of good courage; do not be afraid."
JOSHUA 1:9

_____

_____

REFLECT ON THIS

Turn to Deuteronomy 8:2. How did forty years in the desert prepare the Israelites to enter the promised land?

_____

_____

_____

Study Romans 6:1–23. Why do you think Joshua instructed the people to sanctify themselves in Joshua 3:5?

_____

_____

_____

When the people in your life watch your walk with the Lord, what do they see? How are you trusting God's promises for tomorrow?

_____

_____

_____

CAUGHT IN THE SIN CYCLE

JUDGES

In those days there was no king in Israel; everyone did what was right in his own eyes.

JUDGES 17:6

JUDGES 2:7 STATES, "SO THE PEOPLE served the LORD all the days of Joshua." But within one generation, everything changed. Rather than cleansing Canaan of its pagan tribes, the Israelites allowed some to remain. Soon, the culture devolved into paganism, and everyone was doing "what was right in his own eyes."

From ritualistic orgies to human sacrifice, the Canaanites' expression of Baalism was as debased as anything this world has known. God ordered Israel to "utterly overthrow them" because He knew His people could not coexist with such wickedness (Exodus 23:23–24). But when the covenant community failed to obey completely, they passed through four stages of spiritual decline.

STAGE 1: TOLERATION. According to the book of Judges, several tribes of Israel failed to drive the Canaanites out of their territory. Instead of obeying the Lord's explicit instructions, they chose to tolerate their new neighbors. Accepting people for who God created them to be is one thing, but permitting immorality is an entirely different matter.

STAGE 2: ASSIMILATION. Not only did Israel tolerate the Canaanites; they also began to dwell among them. As they began to adopt Canaanite beliefs and traditions, they lost their unique identity.

STAGE 3: IMITATION. Eventually, cultural assimilation gave way to religious imitation. Judges 2:11 says, "Then the children of Israel did evil in the sight of the LORD, and served the Baals." By commingling the Canaanite gods with their God, the Israelites began to practice pluralism, syncretism, and idolatry.

STAGE 4: REJECTION. No longer acknowledging the one true God, they broke every command, preferring the worship of Ashtoreth and Baal to the worship of Almighty God. Israel's disobedience led to a recurring cycle of sin, judgment, repentance, and deliverance.

A VERSE TO WRITE

When all that generation had been gathered to their fathers, another generation arose after them who did not know the LORD nor the work which He had done for Israel.

JUDGES 2:10

REFLECT ON THIS

What attributes of God do you see in Judges 2:14–18?

_____

_____

_____

What was the role of the Old Testament judges? (Judges 2:14–18)

_____

_____

_____

What signs of pluralism do you see in the church today? (2 Timothy 3:1–5)

_____

_____

_____

Pray and ask God to help your local church remain faithful to sound doctrine.

_____

_____

_____

A PICTURE OF REDEMPTION

RUTH

Now this is the genealogy of Perez: Perez . . . Hezron . . . Ram . . . Amminadab . . .
Nahshon . . . Salmon . . . Boaz . . . Obed . . . Jesse . . . David.

RUTH 4:18–22

RUTH'S STORY BEGINS WITH A REGRETTABLE decision she had no part in making. Facing famine in Judah, a man named Elimelech decided to relocate his family to Moab, a land known for its immorality and idolatry, rather than trusting God for His provision. During this stay, both of Elimelech and Naomi's sons married Moabite women—Ruth being one. In time, all three men in the family died, leaving the women barren and destitute.

Naomi decided to return to Judah, which presented Ruth with a fateful choice: Would she stay in Moab or go with Naomi to live among God's covenant people? Ruth chose to leave her homeland to care for Naomi. What she couldn't have known was that her decision to leave Moab would place her at the center of God's redemptive plan.

Ruth's faith walk did not end when she left Moab. Upon her arrival in Bethlehem, Ruth worked hard to provide for Naomi, adapted to Hebrew customs, and followed Naomi's counsel. Her response: "All that you [Naomi] say to me I will do" (Ruth 3:5). Ruth's humility and love for Naomi not only honored the Lord but also caught the attention of the man who would become her kinsman-redeemer: Boaz.

> While we might not enjoy reading Scripture's genealogies as much as other passages, God placed them in Scripture for a reason.

Through their union, Obed was born. He became the father of Jesse, and Jesse was the father of David. While we might not enjoy reading Scripture's genealogies as much as other passages, God placed them in Scripture for a reason. Here in the book of Ruth, we find vital details about God's commitment to fulfilling the promise He made to Abraham in Genesis 12 and how it extends to those who place their faith in Him today.

A VERSE TO WRITE

The Lord repay your work, and a full reward be given you by the Lord God of Israel, under whose wings you have come for refuge.

RUTH 2:12

_____

_____

_____

REFLECT ON THIS

According to Ruth 1:1, when did Ruth and Naomi live? What do you know about that era?

_____

_____

_____

Compare the genealogy in Ruth 4:18–22 with Matthew 1:1–17. What similarities do you find? What does this say about God's view of Ruth?

_____

_____

_____

No matter who you are, where you've been, or what you've done, God can override the circumstances of your life and give you a purpose in His plan of redemption. What situations do you need to entrust to His care?

_____

_____

_____

A MAN AFTER GOD'S OWN HEART

1 AND 2 SAMUEL

*The Lord has sought for Himself a man after His own heart, and the
Lord has commanded him to be commander over His people.*

1 SAMUEL 13:14

ONE BY ONE, THE JUDGES HAD COME to power, presiding over the people. They could deliver Israel from peril caused by their wickedness, but they were powerless to deliver the Israelites from the evil within their own hearts. Finally, the last godly judge, Samuel, retired. His sons succeeded him, but they "turned aside after dishonest gain, took bribes, and perverted justice" (1 Samuel 8:3).

Rather than asking God for a new judge, the people asked for a king. This request grieved Samuel, but God directed him to grant their appeal and anoint Saul. Why would God honor such a request? In Hosea, the Lord said, "I gave you a king in My anger, and took him away in My wrath" (13:11). God gave the people what they wanted, but Saul was not what they needed.

While Saul's troubled reign ended with his suicide, David was

> *The king's heart is in the hand of the LORD, like the rivers of water; He turns it wherever He wishes.*
>
> PROVERBS 21:1

hand-selected by God. Scripture gives us several clues about his qualifications.

DAVID WAS A MAN AFTER GOD'S HEART. Although he didn't follow God perfectly, David loved the things God loved. He yearned to build a permanent dwelling place for the Almighty. He wrote psalms of worship. He was passionate about serving the Lord.

DAVID HAD A SERVANT'S HEART. Psalm 89:19–20 gives us a glimpse of God's thoughts: "I have raised up a warrior. I have selected him from the common people to be king. I have found my servant David" (NLT). David was tough enough to be king but humble enough to serve ordinary citizens.

DAVID WAS A PRIVATE PERSON. David didn't spend his time in the city but in the hills on the outskirts of Bethlehem. When he rescued his sheep from the mouths of bears and lions, there was no audience. But like Moses before him, David's time in the wilderness prepared his heart for a place of leadership.

A VERSE TO WRITE

For Your word's sake, and according to Your own heart, You have done all these great things, to make Your servant know them.

2 SAMUEL 7:21

_____

_____

_____

REFLECT ON THIS

Read Matthew 20:20–28. According to Jesus, who is responsible for assigning honor to an individual? What qualifications does He give for leadership?

_____

_____

_____

Read Proverbs 16:18. How did pride affect David's reign? How has it affected your life and ministry?

_____

_____

_____

Read 2 Samuel 7:12–16. What did God promise David? How does the fact that it was promised to come to fruition after David died speak to David's humility and the legacy that would stretch far beyond his lifetime? What kind of legacy will you leave behind, and will it honor God?

_____

_____

_____

HEARING GOD'S MESSAGES

1 AND 2 KINGS

How long will you falter between two opinions? If the LORD
is God, follow Him; but if Baal, follow him.

1 KINGS 18:21

WHEN GOD WAS ISRAEL'S ACKNOWLEDGED KING, He
led the nation spiritually, and the judges led the nation physically.
Once Israel became a monarchy, God began appointing prophets
to communicate His truth to the kings as they led God's people.
The presence of an Old Testament prophet was a signal of a king's
failure. Whenever a king began to fail morally, God introduced a
prophet to guide the nation spiritually.

The word we translate "prophet" comes from the Hebrew *nabi*,
meaning "spokesman." An Old Testament prophet was one who
spoke on behalf of God. He wasn't there to give speeches or write
books. He was there to deliver a message, which the recipient usually did not want to hear.

After King David died, the Lord granted his son Solomon

supernatural wisdom, wealth, honor, and a long life. The entire nation prospered. Because of Solomon's remarkable insight, there was little need for a prophet until the latter years of his reign. As he aged, the glorious image of his wisdom faded. He began chasing after foreign wives and foreign gods. When the Lord could no longer rely on Solomon to rule wisely, He raised up the prophet Ahijah.

Things only got worse after Solomon's death. The ten Northern tribes of Israel seceded from the two Southern tribes of Judah. Every Northern king did evil in the sight of the Lord, as did most of Judah's kings. Both kingdoms spiraled into such immorality that God allowed neighboring empires to conquer them. But through it all, He never stopped raising up prophets to call the kings and nations to repentance.

A VERSE TO WRITE

The children of Israel had sinned against the LORD their God, who had brought them up out of the land of Egypt, from under the hand of Pharaoh king of Egypt; and they had feared other gods.

2 KINGS 17:7

_____

_____

_____

_____

_____

REFLECT ON THIS

First Kings 11 describes Solomon's sins and their consequences. How did his sin affect his family and the nation?

_____

_____

_____

From your reading of 1 and 2 Kings, what did you notice about the prophets' response to adversity? How does it demonstrate their humanity? What about their commitment to God's message?

_____

_____

_____

_____

Read 2 Kings 20:1–6. How does God's interaction with Hezekiah differ from the way God interacted with many of the other kings in this book? What does this show us about the power of the prayers of a faithful servant of God who heeds His warnings?

_____

_____

_____

_____

GOD'S TRUSTWORTHY WORDS FOR HIS PEOPLE

1 AND 2 CHRONICLES

❧

"If My people who are called by My name will humble themselves, and
pray and seek My face, and turn from their wicked ways, then I will
hear from heaven, and will forgive their sin and heal their land."

2 CHRONICLES 7:14

THE BOOKS OF CHRONICLES COVER the same era as
the books of 1 and 2 Kings but with a different emphasis. While 1
and 2 Kings provide a clear picture of *why* the people were exiled,
1 and 2 Chronicles assure the returning exiles that they are still
the people of God. These books offer hope by emphasizing Israel's
glorious heritage, God's presence, and His enduring promises.

In 1 Chronicles 29, we find Israel gathered as a nation, filling
the temple treasury with generous offerings given from "a loyal

> *The object of the Bible is not to tell how good men are, but how bad men can become good.*
> DWIGHT L. MOODY

heart" (v. 9). Seven years later, the glory of the Lord filled the temple as Solomon dedicated it, and the people worshiped. The Lord appeared to Solomon, saying, "I have chosen this Temple and set it apart to be holy—a place where my name will be honored forever. I will always watch over it, for it is dear to my heart" (2 Chronicles 7:16 NLT). But He also warned them: if Israel were to turn away from Him, God would uproot the people from their land and reject the temple.

Over the next three hundred years, the nation became divided and departed from its spiritual heritage. Faithful to His word, God allowed the Babylonians to destroy Jerusalem and the temple in 586 BC. Those who survived were deported to Babylon.

One thing we never have to worry about with God is broken promises. His words are trustworthy and eternal; they reflect His character. After Solomon finished dedicating the temple in Jerusalem, he declared that not one word of God's promises had gone unfulfilled. That declaration remains as true today as it was then. God keeps His promises.

A VERSE TO WRITE

"His throne shall be established forever."
1 CHRONICLES 17:14

_____

_____

REFLECT ON THIS

Read 2 Chronicles 7:12–22. What instructions, promises, and warnings do you find?

_____

_____

_____

_____

_____

Read John 2:13–22. Then read 1 Corinthians 3:16–17. Where is God's temple now? How do the promises and warnings of 2 Chronicles relate to God's people today?

_____

_____

_____

_____

_____

PRAYERS TO GUIDE US

EZRA AND NEHEMIAH

I was very much afraid. . . . Then I prayed to the God of heaven, and I answered the king.
NEHEMIAH 2:2, 4–5 NIV

SEVENTY YEARS AFTER JERUSALEM FELL to Babylon,
Nehemiah discovered that the once-glorious city lay in ruins. He
spent the next several days fasting and seeking God's guidance.
Not long after, he had an opportunity to ask King Artaxerxes for
permission to rebuild the city. It was a bold request, but Nehemiah
succeeded because God had planted the dream in his heart.

While Nehemiah planned the reconstruction of the city walls,
Ezra spearheaded the rebuilding of the temple. Both men provided
remarkable spiritual and visionary leadership as the people picked
up the broken pieces of their heritage. In Nehemiah's book, we find
details of his prayer life that can guide us today.

PREPARE YOUR HEART FOR GOD'S PLAN. When
Nehemiah felt a burden in his heart, he started praying about it.
Notice these two telling phrases: Nehemiah stated that God "put

[it] in my heart" to rebuild the city walls, and later he said, "My God put it into my heart" to organize the people (Nehemiah 2:12 NIV; 7:5). Nehemiah was sensitive to the Lord's guidance.

COMMIT TO PASSIONATE, ONGOING PRAYER. As soon as Nehemiah heard about Jerusalem's condition, he "sat down and wept, and mourned for many days . . . fasting and praying before the God of heaven" (Nehemiah 1:4). Prayer is the divine energy that goes into His plans, but we must learn to pray with enthusiasm, persistence, and faith, as Nehemiah did.

PREPARE FOR GOD TO DO THINGS HIS WAY. As God drops seeds of aspiration into our minds and we begin to pray over them, we'll learn to trust His blueprint for success. We need to plan, but we also need to be ready for God to lead in ways we may not anticipate. We must follow by faith.

CELEBRATE GOD'S FAITHFULNESS. Once the city walls were complete, Ezra gathered the people at the Water Gate. They dedicated the wall, worshiped the Lord, made sacrifices, and rejoiced. By starting in prayer, they ended in victory.

A VERSE TO WRITE

"If you return to Me, and keep My commandments and do them . . . I will gather them from there, and bring them to the place which I have chosen as a dwelling for My name."
NEHEMIAH 1:9

_____

_____

_____

REFLECT ON THIS

"ACTS" is an acronym for four elements of prayer: adoration, confession, thanksgiving, and supplication (requests). How does Nehemiah 1:5–11 reflect these elements?

_____

_____

_____

Read Ezra 10:14. Is there any unconfessed sin standing between you and God? How will you confront it?

_____

_____

_____

Nehemiah knowingly put his life in danger when he petitioned the king because he trusted God's leading. How is God calling you to step out of your comfort zone? How will you respond?

_____

_____

_____

THE LORD'S PERFECT JUSTICE

ESTHER

Who knows whether you have come to the kingdom for such a time as this?

ESTHER 4:14

AFTER THE BABYLONIANS TOOK THE JEWS into exile, the Medo-Persian Empire conquered Babylon and inherited their Jewish captives. One wave of Jews returned to Jerusalem, but many stayed behind or dispersed to other locations. Esther was among those who remained in Persia.

When the reigning king, Ahasuerus, deposed his queen, he had to find a suitable replacement. His attendants presented beautiful young women from every corner of the kingdom for the king's consideration, including Esther. Against this unlikely backdrop, Ahasuerus selected Esther to be the new queen of Persia.

The book of Esther never mentions God's name, but His providence is evident on every page. Esther's position in the palace enabled Esther and her cousin, Mordecai, to prevent the king's assassination. Later, Mordecai counseled Esther when Haman, a palace advisor, attempted to wipe out the Jews. And together,

Esther and Mordecai devised a plan to save their people.

The story twists and turns like a Hollywood thriller, but in the end, Esther saved herself and her people from certain death. Haman ended up hanging from the gallows he built for Mordecai. And the very last verse of the book tells us, "Mordecai the Jew was second to King Ahasuerus, and was great among the Jews and well received by the multitude of his brethren, seeking the good of his people and speaking peace to all his countrymen" (10:3).

We might call it poetic justice, but it's the Lord's justice. Through it all, God was working behind the scenes, ordering events, and controlling circumstances when everything appeared to be out of control. He had a plan for His people then, and He has a plan for us now. His invisible hand works all things "together for good to those who love God, to those who are the called according to His purpose" (Romans 8:28).

A VERSE TO WRITE

Then King Ahasuerus said . . . "Indeed, I have given Esther the house of Haman . . . because he tried to lay his hand on the Jews."

ESTHER 8:7

_____

_____

_____

REFLECT ON THIS

In Esther chapter 4, how did Esther discern God's will?

_____

_____

_____

Read Esther 4:13–16. How will you commit to following God wherever He leads you?

_____

_____

_____

Read Esther 9:13. How has retaliation damaged your relationships?

_____

_____

_____

_____

POETRY AND WISDOM

———— ∾ ————

JOB, PSALMS, PROVERBS, ECCLESIASTES, AND SONG OF SOLOMON

———— ∾ ————

THE POETIC BOOKS ARE ALSO KNOWN as "wisdom literature" and contain poetry and wisdom from the psalmists, King David, and King Solomon. To read these words is to read words that once echoed off the walls of the temple in Jerusalem. Reading them keeps us oriented to God's priorities and wisdom.

WHY, LORD?

JOB

———— ❧ ————

Though He slay me, yet will I trust Him. . . . I know that my Redeemer lives.

JOB 13:15; 19:25

AS THE FIRST POETIC BOOK, Job strays from the storyline of previous books to give us a glimpse into one man's life. Unlike Esther, Job's story does not affect the future of Israel. We don't even know when it was written. But Job has helped generations of believers to trust God through difficult times.

When we meet Job, God has blessed him with a wife, ten children, and great wealth. By the end of the second chapter, Satan has stripped him of his children, health, and fortune. For reasons we cannot entirely understand, God allowed Job to be severely tried and tested. But these chapters contain three valuable principles about enduring trials.

PATIENCE. James 5:11 is the only New Testament verse to mention Job, and it praises his endurance. Satan had hoped that Job would become impatient with God and give up. Instead, Job became impatient with himself and his friends. He never lost faith in the Lord.

PERSPECTIVE. When it comes to trials and life itself, perspective is everything. In chapter 2, Job asked his wife, "Shall we indeed accept good from God, and shall we not accept adversity?" (v. 10). Knowing that he had received many undeserved blessings from God helped Job to trust the Lord during difficult times.

PERSISTENCE. Job 2:10 makes this stunning statement: "In all this Job did not sin with his lips." By his example, we discover how to respond to difficult times, even if we do not understand why God permits the trial. We have a choice: we can get bitter, or we can get better. We cannot change our circumstances, but we can control our response to them. Even when everything is falling apart, we can stand firm in our commitment and faith in Almighty God.

A VERSE TO WRITE

The LORD restored Job's losses when he prayed for his friends.
Indeed the LORD gave Job twice as much as he had before.

JOB 42:10

_____

_____

_____

_____

_____

REFLECT ON THIS

Read James 1:2–4. In your own words, summarize the lesson to be learned from this passage. Describe the fruit that patience will bear in the believer's life.

_____

_____

_____

Spend some time in prayer, and ask God to open your eyes to the ways Satan has influenced your perception of Him.

_____

_____

_____

Read Job 4:7–11 and Romans 3:21–26. What shortcomings do you find in the principle of retribution? How is God's plan better?

_____

_____

_____

SING A BEAUTIFUL SONG

PSALMS OF PRAISE

Serve the LORD with gladness; come before His presence with singing.
PSALM 100:2

AT THE VERY HEART OF THE BIBLE lies the book of Psalms, the ancient hymnbook of God's people. It teaches us to praise God for His greatness, goodness, and glory. In just five verses, Psalm 100 shows us why we should worship God, and it outlines six ways for us to praise Him.

OBEDIENTLY. The psalm issues six commands regarding worship: "Make a joyful shout. . . . Serve the LORD . . . come before His presence. . . . Know that the LORD, He is God. . . . Enter into His gates. . . . Be thankful" (vv. 1–4). While not everyone is gifted to sing in the choir, praising God in worship is a matter of obedience.

BEAUTIFULLY. When it comes to God, your voice is not nearly as important as your motivation. This form of beauty comes from an "upright" heart (Psalm 111:1). No matter your skill level, God will accept any song offered to Him out of love and devotion.

MUSICALLY. In biblical times, musical instruments often accompanied worship. Psalm 150 tells us to praise the Lord with trumpets, lutes, harps, timbrels, stringed instruments, flutes, and loud and clashing cymbals. Today, the instruments have changed, but the principle remains—praise Him with what you've got!

CREATIVELY. Sometimes it's tempting to settle into a routine and sing the same old songs. But Psalm 33:3 commands us, "Sing to Him a new song." Our worship should come from the freshness of our hearts and reflect our ongoing appreciation for God's grace in our lives.

SKILLFULLY. God deserves our best. Just as we offer the first tenth of our income as a tithe, God expects our praise to represent the firstfruits of our effort. Slipups will happen, but they should not occur because of a lack of effort on our part.

JOYFULLY. There are occasions for somber, contemplative praise, but Psalm 100:1 tells us there is a time to shout joyfully. Can you imagine if we all showed up at church with the same enthusiasm we bring to a ball game? Our exuberance for praising God should be no less than our praise for human activities.

A VERSE TO WRITE

I will sing to the LORD, because He has dealt bountifully with me.

PSALM 13:6

REFLECT ON THIS

According to Psalm 33:20–22, what are the results of praise and thanksgiving?

_____

_____

_____

Which of these six aspects of praise do you find easiest? Which is the most challenging? How will you dedicate yourself to giving God your best in worship?

_____

_____

_____

Father God, I thank You for Your Word and Your works. Teach me to be thankful for all that You do for me. This week I commit myself to praise You obediently, beautifully, and joyfully. And as much as I can, I will praise You musically, creatively, and skillfully because You are worthy. You are a great God, and I love You. I trust You to provide the help I need, the joy I seek, and the hope I desire. Lord, I pray that my worship will gladden Your heart. In Jesus' name, amen.

WE DON'T HAVE TO FRET

PSALMS OF INSTRUCTION

Commit your way to the Lord, trust also in Him, and He shall bring it to pass.

PSALM 37:5

THE BIBLE HAS SOMETHING TO SAY about nearly every subject we can imagine, and the Psalms are no exception. They teach us how to live righteously, glorify God, revere His Word, pursue wisdom and forgiveness, plead for justice, and much more. Of all 150 psalms, Psalm 37 is my favorite. In the first eight verses, it tells us, "Do not fret," three times.

How do we keep from worrying? This passage outlines five choices we can make to keep from worrying: "Trust in the Lord, and do good. . . . Delight yourself also in the Lord. . . . Commit your way to the Lord, trust also in Him. . . . Rest in the Lord . . . wait patiently for Him" (vv. 3–5, 7). We can do nothing about tomorrow, so we wait for God—for His timing, guidance, and provision. He is already orchestrating tomorrow's circumstances for our benefit. Our part is simply to wait.

In the New Testament, one of the biggest worriers was Peter. When the Lord called Peter out on the water, he worried about drowning. At other times, he worried about Jesus paying His taxes, who would betray Jesus, and the suffering Jesus would endure. When anxiety got to him in the garden of Gethsemane, he even cut off the ear of a servant of the high priest.

Peter often worried about what would happen. But as he got to know the Lord better, he learned to trust Him with tomorrow. "Give all your worries and cares to God, for he cares about you" (1 Peter 5:7 NLT). Who wrote that? The worrier did. Looking back at his experiences with the Lord, Peter could see that worrying never solved anything, but trusting the Lord solved everything.

We face the same choice. We can worry, or we can step into each new day with confidence in the Lord's power and promises.

> *Knowledge of the Bible never comes by intuition. It can only be obtained by diligent, regular, daily, attentive reading.*
> J. C. RYLE

A VERSE TO WRITE

Search me, O God, and know my heart; try me, and know my anxieties.

PSALM 139:23

_____

_____

_____

REFLECT ON THIS

Read Psalm 37:1–8. What does the passage instruct us not to fret about? Why don't we need to worry?

_____

_____

_____

Read Psalm 139. The editors of the New King James Version have titled this chapter "God's Perfect Knowledge of Man." How does understanding God's perfect knowledge help you face uncertainty?

_____

_____

_____

Read Psalm 119:33–56 aloud, if possible, and make it your prayer to the Lord.

_____

_____

_____

SEEING PAST YOUR PAIN

PSALMS OF LAMENT

———— ∾ ————

How long, O Lord? Will You forget me forever?
PSALM 13:1

DAVID'S LIFE WAS COMPLICATED. As a boy, he battled wild animals in the rugged hills outside of Bethlehem. While still a youth, he killed Goliath, Israel's chief adversary, only to be hunted by King Saul. At least three of his sons died during his lifetime, including Absalom, who tried to usurp his throne. Stunning losses often tempered David's thrilling victories.

In his darkest moments, David penned psalms that not only provided a window into his suffering but also teach us how to trust God when our world falls apart. He pleaded with the Lord in ways we sometimes are afraid to voice. This body of writing is known as the psalms of lament, Psalm 13 being one example.

After pouring out his pain, David turned his attention from his problems to the very One who was allowing his desperate situation to continue (13:3). By remembering God's promises and past faithfulness, David kept himself from a crisis of faith. Even before his circumstances changed, David's outlook shifted because he found God in the midst of his struggle.

When we are struggling, our emotions can become our greatest enemy. Like David, we begin to believe that God has forgotten us or that He has hidden His face from us. In Psalm 22:1, David cried out, "My God, My God, why have You forsaken Me?" Thousands of years later, Jesus Christ echoed those words as He hung on the cross. God turned His back on His Son so that He would never have to turn His back on us. Scripture reassures us that God cares about our struggles and weaknesses.

During difficult times, we will do well to follow David's example by setting aside our feelings, remembering the Lord's faithfulness, and allowing God to mold us into the person He wants us to be.

A VERSE TO WRITE

But You, O LORD, do not be far from Me; O My Strength, hasten to help Me!
PSALM 22:19

_____

_____

_____

_____

_____

REFLECT ON THIS

David opens Psalm 13 with five questions in a row. Is it all right to question God in times of trial? Why or why not?

_____

_____

_____

Read Jeremiah 20:12–13. Whom does God test? What does He see? How does this truth encourage you?

_____

_____

_____

Compare Jeremiah 20:13 and Psalm 13:6. How do David and Jeremiah respond to God? Are you prepared to offer a similar response, regardless of your circumstances?

_____

_____

_____

WE ARE FREE!

PSALMS OF PROPHECY

⁓

Then I said, "Here I am, I have come—it is written about me in the scroll."

PSALM 40:7 NIV

WHEN JESUS CHRIST STEPPED INTO OUR WORLD, He fulfilled more than three hundred Old Testament prophecies. Someone has calculated that if we organized all the Old Testament predictions and the messianic psalms chronologically, we would have a complete picture of Christ's life without even opening the New Testament. But by studying the Old and New Testaments alongside each other, we gain a fuller understanding of Christ's incarnation.

Psalm 40 provides a remarkable glimpse into our eternal Lord's thoughts and intentions just before His birth in Bethlehem. First, He came to fulfill prophecy. Isaiah 7:14 says, "Behold, the virgin shall conceive and bear a Son." Micah prophesied that "the One to be Ruler in Israel" would come from Bethlehem Ephrathah (5:2). And as far back as Genesis, God's covenant with Abraham predicted that his offspring would bless all people (12:3; 17:19).

According to Psalm 40:8, the second reason Jesus came into the world was to do His Father's will. We find this truth echoed in the New Testament and quoted in Hebrews 10:5 (Matthew 26:39; John 4:34; 6:38).

Finally, Psalm 40 tells us that Jesus came to conquer sin. All the Old Testament animal sacrifices were powerless to save anyone. They only pointed to the coming redemption through Jesus' perfect sacrifice. Before Jesus' death, salvation came through faith in the coming Messiah.

By studying the Old and New Testaments alongside each other, we gain a fuller understanding of Christ's incarnation.

In Jesus Christ, we are free! Because He was both God and man, He could unite us with the Father at the cross. Jesus' precise fulfillment of the messianic prophecies and His perfect obedience to the Father give us great assurance in His victory over death.

A VERSE TO WRITE

I will declare the decree: the LORD has said to Me, "You are My Son, today I have begotten You."

PSALM 2:7

_____

_____

_____

_____

_____

REFLECT ON THIS

Read John 1:1; 8:58; and 10:25–39. What proof do you find for Jesus' deity?

_____

_____

_____

Read Hebrews 10:1–18. In your own words, how is the new covenant superior to the old?

_____

_____

_____

We are privileged to live at a point in history when we can look back at the Messiah's arrival and understand it through the lens of Scripture. Spend some time thanking God that the Savior has come.

_____

_____

_____

A WORD TO THE WISE

PROVERBS

*Incline your ear to wisdom, and apply your heart to understanding . . . then
you will understand the fear of the LORD, and find the knowledge of God.*

PROVERBS 2:2, 5

WHEN SOLOMON BECAME THE KING of Israel, he asked
God for wisdom. This request pleased the Lord so much that He
gave Solomon greater wisdom and understanding than anyone on
earth. Today some of Solomon's insights are preserved in the book
of Proverbs. This fact ought to fill us with great anticipation as we
turn its pages!

No book in the Bible sets forth its purpose with greater clarity
than Proverbs. The opening paragraph tells us that its sayings are
intended to give us wisdom and instruction, help us perceive words
of understanding, and impart prudence and knowledge. Whether
we need guidance for our finances, emotions, attitudes, integrity,
marriage, or anything else, we will find it in Proverbs, particularly
with the illumination of the Holy Spirit.

Repeatedly, Proverbs tells us to "get wisdom." But to do that, we need to answer this question: What is wisdom? Definitions abound, but I suggest that wisdom entails knowing God and His Word and making choices based on that knowledge. Or, as Charles Haddon Spurgeon put it, it is "the right use of knowledge."[6]

The book of Proverbs contains many principles for righteous living, but one permeates all the others: "the fear of the LORD" (1:7). This fear has less to do with quaking in our boots than it does with accepting God's word as final. It's an attitude of "God said it, I believe it, and that settles it." When we come to the place where we revere God's awesome power and authority, we have taken the first step toward wisdom.

Psalms and Proverbs appear side by side in the center of the Bible for a reason. As citizens of heaven, we need a hymnal to fill us with praise to God. As citizens of earth, we need a practical manual for self-improvement in everyday matters. Together these books can help us navigate any storm that comes our way.

A VERSE TO WRITE

Trust in the LORD with all your heart, and lean not on your own understanding.

PROVERBS 3:5

_____

_____

_____

_____

REFLECT ON THIS

What do you learn about "the fear of the LORD" from the following verses? Proverbs 1:29–30; 2:1–5; 8:13; 10:27; 14:26–27; 15:16, 33; 16:6

_____

_____

_____

Read Proverbs 3:5–7. What does it mean to be "wise in your own eyes"?

_____

_____

_____

How can you fear the Lord in your daily life? How can you humble yourself before Him?

_____

_____

_____

PUTTING GOD AT THE CENTER

ECCLESIASTES

—— ❦ ——

Let us hear the conclusion of the whole matter: Fear God and
keep His commandments, for this is man's all.

ECCLESIASTES 12:13

IN OUR DAY, WE TEND TO THINK of a wise person as quiet,
thoughtful, and studious, dispensing wisdom in clipped phrases
from the comfort of a wing-backed chair. But in the Old Testament,
wisdom was synonymous with skill; it was a matter of observation
and implementation.

Like Proverbs, Ecclesiastes was written by Israel's King
Solomon. It records his thoughts after spending many years observ-
ing what worked and what didn't work about life. Having wandered
away from the God of his youth, Solomon found himself to be a
discouraged and regretful old king.

For decades, Solomon tried to find meaning in life through
riches, extravagant and wasteful living, his kingly duties, and
studying the philosophies and beliefs of others. Ecclesiastes is the

history of that ill-fated search, written at the end of his life when he came back to the conclusion of his youth: God is at the center of life, and to ignore Him makes life meaningless. Life is a matter of deceptive illusions when lived apart from God.

It is a shame that Solomon applied his extraordinary skill to search for an answer that he already possessed. God had given Solomon wisdom as a young king; he knew there was no life apart from God (1 Kings 3:4–15). But he spent years proving what he had learned in his youth—and then wrote a book full of his observations.

In the end, Solomon got it right. His "conclusion of the whole matter" is that "man's all" is to "fear God and keep His commandments" (Ecclesiastes 12:13). Almost too late, he validated his reputation as the wisest man in Israel. By studying Ecclesiastes, we can spare ourselves from a lifelong search for meaning and discover true wisdom.

A VERSE TO WRITE

Remember now your Creator in the days of your youth, before the difficult days come.
ECCLESIASTES 12:1

REFLECT ON THIS

Read Ecclesiastes 3:1–8. How would you describe your current "season" of life? How will you commit to spending each moment wisely?

_____

_____

_____

Read Revelation 2:5. How does Ecclesiastes reflect Solomon's journey of restoration, repentance, and repetition?

_____

_____

_____

In the New King James Version, Solomon addressed "my son" twenty-three times in Proverbs, and he concluded Ecclesiastes with the same address (12:12). It is easy to imagine the aged king yearning to spare his children from his mistakes. Would you want your children to follow in your footsteps? What change(s) will you make today for the sake of future generations?

_____

_____

_____

EXPRESSING LOVE

SONG OF SOLOMON

Many waters cannot quench love, nor can the floods drown it.
SONG OF SOLOMON 8:7

THE SONG OF SOLOMON TAKES US BACK to Solomon's glory days when he was a young, virile king with a heart that beat passionately for God and the woman he loved. Composed of fifteen reflections written as lyric poetry, this unlikely love story between a king and a commoner provides a template for understanding God's purpose and design for marriage. Among other things, it provides biblical principles for giving and receiving love through the medium of healthy communication.

PRAISE. It is impossible to show love without using the principle of praise. When we are in love, we say, "Let me count the ways." In Song of Solomon 1:9–10, Solomon quiets Shulamith's insecurities through genuine, heartfelt praise and encouragement. In the next verse, he takes it to another level by inviting others to praise her, shifting the focus from "I" to "we."

Shulamith responds with praise for Solomon. The effect is like a contest in which the two try to "outdo one another in showing honor" (Romans 12:10 ESV). There is tremendous healing power in magnifying all that is good in our loved ones.

PASSION. Song of Solomon 1:12 reads, "While the king is at his table, my spikenard sends forth its fragrance." The word *spikenard* doesn't quite carry the music of poetry, nor does it sound like a name we would assign to a perfume. Yet in the Bible, this is the name of a very precious fragrance. In verse 13, Shulamith also talks about myrrh as a rich, fragrant reminder of Solomon, who held a royal place in her nation and heart. A king deserves royal fragrance, and the aromas of spikenard and myrrh send that message.

Solomon and Shulamith held nothing back as they expressed their love for each other with all five senses. They have given us a terrific example of how a couple can creatively express their love for each other.

A VERSE TO WRITE

How fair and how pleasant you are, O love, with your delights!
SONG OF SOLOMON 7:6

_____

_____

_____

_____

_____

REFLECT ON THIS

How does Song of Solomon help you to understand God's design for marriage?

_____

_____

_____

_____

_____

_____

Read Song of Solomon 2:15. If you are married, are there any "little foxes" that are nibbling away at your relationship?

_____

_____

_____

_____

_____

BOOKS OF PROPHECY

———— ❧ ————

ISAIAH, JEREMIAH, LAMENTATIONS, EZEKIEL, DANIEL, HOSEA, JOEL, AMOS, OBADIAH, JONAH, MICAH, NAHUM, HABAKKUK, ZEPHANIAH, HAGGAI, ZECHARIAH, AND MALACHI

———— ❧ ————

THE LAST SEVENTEEN BOOKS of the Old Testament are prophetic. They warn the people of Israel that hardship will follow their disobedience. But these books offer hope as well: God promises spiritual blessing, protection, guidance, and vows that He will send the Messiah to rescue His people.

KEEP YOUR CHIN UP!

ISAIAH

*The everlasting God, the LORD, the Creator of the ends of the earth, neither
faints nor is weary. His understanding is unsearchable. He gives power to
the weak, and to those who have no might He increases strength.*

ISAIAH 40:28–29

ISAIAH MARKS THE BEGINNING of the prophetic books.
After beginning his ministry around 740 BC, the prophet witnessed the final years of the Northern Kingdom of Israel and
warned Judah of a similar judgment. The last part of Isaiah speaks
to the future exiles and contains some of the most comforting passages in the Bible. Isaiah portrays God as both our majestic Lord
and our Suffering Servant—the Source of our strength.

It's a natural law that we can give away only what we possess.
And because God Himself is strong, He can give strength to the
weak. Today's passage contains a veritable list of the attributes of
God. He is eternal, sovereign, omnipotent, immutable, omniscient,
merciful, and gracious. He is more than sufficient when it comes to

imparting power and strength to us. His strength empowers us to soar—to rise above the busyness and noise of life on earth and live with peace and contentment. But to draw on His power, we must wait upon Him.

Having predicted the Babylonian captivity (chapter 39), Isaiah then wrote to the future exiles (chapters 40–66). In the face of an uncertain future, they would need to have faith in God's sovereignty and His plan of redemption. It would require their confession and spiritual renewal, but Isaiah predicted that God would deliver His people from Babylon and, more importantly, from the tyranny of sin.

When we most need God, we find great motivation by learning to wait upon Him for strength. The problem is that most of us have been immersed in our culture for so long that we don't realize how weak we are. But as soon as we begin to wait upon Him, we discover renewed perspective, protection, provision, and power.

A VERSE TO WRITE

The LORD will guide you continually, and satisfy your soul in drought.
ISAIAH 58:11

_____

_____

_____

_____

_____

REFLECT ON THIS

Read Psalm 119:165; Isaiah 26:3; John 16:33; Romans 5:1; 1 Corinthians 1:30; Ephesians 2:4–6; Philippians 4:4–7; Colossians 3:15. What reasons do you find for having peace regardless of your circumstances?

_____

_____

_____

_____

Read Isaiah 5:1–10 and Psalm 80:8–18. How did Israel's disobedience affect other nations?

_____

_____

_____

_____

Read Isaiah 30:15–17. Is there an area of your life that you need to recommit to God's strength?

_____

_____

_____

CONFIDENCE IN HARD TIMES

JEREMIAH

❧

I hurt with the hurt of my people. I mourn and am overcome with grief.
JEREMIAH 8:21 NLT

THE PROPHET JEREMIAH MINISTERED during the last forty years of Judah's history, from the thirteenth year of King Josiah to the destruction of the nation. In my estimation, he is the loneliest man to walk through the pages of the Old Testament. His loneliness and depression stemmed from the spiritual decline of his country.

It became increasingly apparent to Jeremiah that his preaching was going unheeded. It got to the point that he felt like keeping his mouth shut and not continuing to minister. But he couldn't do it, for the Word of God was "in my bones" (Jeremiah 20:9). He just had to let it out. God's message demanded to be heard. As Paul put it in the New Testament, "Woe is me if I do not preach the gospel!" (1 Corinthians 9:16).

Jeremiah wanted out of his job, but he couldn't leave it. There was something greater than himself driving him forward. He knew that God had called him to preach repentance to Israel. God had implanted His Word within Jeremiah and installed him as a prophet. No matter how much he wanted to get away from the ministry, he had to continue because it was God who had given him the task.

Have you ever read about Jeremiah's call? God told him, "Before I formed you in the womb I knew you; before you were born I sanctified you; I ordained you a prophet to the nations. . . . For you shall go to all to whom I send you, and whatever I command you, you shall speak" (1:5, 7). Notice the prominence of the perpendicular pronoun "I": "I formed you . . . I knew you . . . I sanctified you . . . I ordained you . . . I command you." Jeremiah knew he wasn't in Israel by his design; he was there because God had placed him there.

No one is exempt from experiencing circumstances that lead to discouragement. It can be tempting to insulate or isolate ourselves, but we can keep discouragement from turning to despair with preparation. Conviction, confidence, and commitment encourage steadfastness in life.

A VERSE TO WRITE

I know the thoughts that I think toward you, says the LORD, thoughts
of peace and not of evil, to give you a future and a hope.
JEREMIAH 29:11

_____

_____

REFLECT ON THIS

In Jeremiah 3:6; 5:30–31; 8:20; 9:1; 13:17; and 20:14–18, what factors contributed to Jeremiah's despair?

_____

_____

_____

What motivated Jeremiah to keep going? (Jeremiah 1:5, 7; 17:7–8; 20:7–9, 11; 29:11)

_____

_____

_____

Read Jeremiah 20:13. In the context of Jeremiah's depression, what basis did he find for praising the Lord?

_____

_____

_____

NO MATTER WHAT, GOD IS FAITHFUL

LAMENTATIONS

———— ❦ ————

Through the LORD's mercies we are not consumed, because His compassions
fail not. They are new every morning; great is Your faithfulness.

LAMENTATIONS 3:22–23

JERUSALEM HAD BEEN UNDER SIEGE for eighteen months. Cut off from any outside provisions, people were dying of starvation and thirst. It got so bad that people killed and ate their children to stay alive (Lamentations 4:10). Amid this devastation, Jeremiah wrote the book of Lamentations.

It must have been horrible for a godly prophet to watch God's judgment fall on Jerusalem. Yet Lamentations holds one of the key verses on God's faithfulness in all the Bible. Jeremiah remembered God's faithfulness, and it gave him hope!

As he penned the words about new mercies, all Jeremiah could see with his eyes was devastation. But with the eyes of faith, he could see God's faithfulness. Often in life, we will see with our physical eyes only that which appears to confound our perception of who God is. Like Jeremiah, we need eyes of faith to see beyond our circumstances.

Life is filled with challenges seen and unseen. The only way we will be able to get through them is if we depend on the faithfulness of God. His constancy becomes a source of courage to all who trust in Him. We need to do what Jeremiah did: remember God's faithfulness and how He has delivered His people, including us, in the past.

God's faithfulness is at the core of His revelation in Scripture. In the Old Testament, "faithful" comes from the Hebrew root *aman*, from which we get our word *amen*. The root means "to confirm, support," and *amen* means "so be it." Every one of God's promises is "amen," confirmed and certain.

In a world where people often break promises as quickly as they are made, there is still One whose word is His bond. He is trustworthy, faithful in all things, and He does not change by time or circumstance. Part of God's character is His faithfulness, and we worship Him for it.

A VERSE TO WRITE

Turn us back to You, O LORD, and we will be restored; renew our days as of old.

LAMENTATIONS 5:21

_____

_____

_____

REFLECT ON THIS

What do the following verses reveal about God's faithfulness?
1 Corinthians 10:13; 2 Thessalonians 3:3; 2 Timothy 2:13; 1 John 1:9

_____

_____

_____

Read Psalm 91:15, and list the three promises God gives to those who
call upon Him.

_____

_____

_____

Read Lamentations 1:12–13. Are there matters about which you would
like to lament before the Lord? Let the book of Lamentations be your
model as you commit your grievances to Almighty God.

_____

_____

_____

GOD OPENS DOORS

EZEKIEL

*"I will give you a new heart and put a new spirit within you; I will take
the heart of stone out of your flesh and give you a heart of flesh."*

EZEKIEL 36:26

WE OFTEN NEED A FRESH START after enduring disappointment. As a young man, Ezekiel had dedicated himself to be a priest when he turned thirty. But when he was about twenty-five, Ezekiel was seized and taken to Babylon, and he never saw the temple again. When his thirtieth birthday came, he must have struggled with questions of "why" and "if only."

That's when God appeared to him as he was among the exiles by the Kebar River. Ezekiel looked up and saw remarkable visions of God—the throne of God surrounded by angelic beings. Amid the strange and apocalyptic vision described in Ezekiel 1, God called the thirty-year-old exile to be a mighty prophet. Ezekiel's later years were far from what he had envisioned as a young man, but God gave him a vision that stretched to the end of the earth's days.

O. S. Hawkins has written:

> While God used Jeremiah to warn the people of Jerusalem of their coming destruction, He used Ezekiel to be His prophetic voice during their days of exile in Babylonian captivity. Along with Daniel and Revelation, the book of Ezekiel is filled with visions, dreams, symbolism, allegories, prophecies, and parables. God spoke through the various visions of Ezekiel to remind His people that even though they were far away from their Holy City, they were still subject to God's laws and statutes. Ezekiel thundered forth message after message of warnings to God's people, but he wrapped each of them in a ribbon of hope.[7]

To this day, the book of Ezekiel adds tremendously to our understanding of the present and the future. It tells us that God has a vision for our future even when we feel like exiles in a land of failure. Circumstances cannot and should not keep us from speaking God's words to our generation. If one door closes, it's because God intends to open another.

A VERSE TO WRITE

Thus says the Lord God: "On the day that I cleanse you from all your iniquities,
I will also enable you to dwell in the cities, and the ruins shall be rebuilt."

EZEKIEL 36:33

REFLECT ON THIS

Read Ezekiel 28:11–19. In your own words, how does pride interfere with your ability to serve the Lord?

_____

_____

_____

_____

What does Ezekiel tell us about Israel's spiritual rebirth in the latter days? (Ezekiel 36:24–28; 37:14, 26–27)

_____

_____

_____

Read Ezekiel 2:7–3:9. Do you find it more natural to speak with conviction and strength or compassion and empathy? Ask God to empower you in your area(s) of weakness and equip you for effective ministry.

_____

_____

_____

UNTIL JESUS COMES AGAIN

DANIEL

He [God] changes the times and the seasons; He removes kings and raises up kings;
He gives wisdom to the wise and knowledge to those who have understanding.

DANIEL 2:21

MORE THAN TWENTY-FIVE HUNDRED years ago, Daniel
stood in front of King Nebuchadnezzar, the most powerful ruler in
the world, and delivered a panoramic overview of world history—
from his own time up to the second coming of Israel's Messiah,
Jesus Christ.

Daniel's prophetic presentations centered on two dreams. One
was a dream of Nebuchadnezzar that Daniel interpreted (Daniel
2), and the other was Daniel's own dream (Daniel 7). While we
will focus our study on the king's dream, both visions had the same
purpose: to communicate God's plan for elevating His kingdom
over all the kingdoms of the earth.

In his dream, Nebuchadnezzar envisioned an enormous statue
with five sections, each representing an empire that would rule the

world before Christ's millennial reign. The statue's golden head signified Babylon. The silver breast and arms depicted Medo-Persia, and the belly and thighs of bronze represented Greece. Its iron legs symbolized Rome.

History confirms that each of these kingdoms succeeded the other just as Nebuchadnezzar's dream predicted. Still, the final empire—the feet of iron and clay—remains in the future as a revived version of the Roman Empire. Iron indicates strength, while clay suggests the subjective will of the people involved. Many people groups will unite under ten leaders or powers, with one individual holding ultimate authority.

We refer to this ruler as the Antichrist. He will rise as the leader of the revived Roman Empire and oppose the God of heaven and His people. While we may not be able to imagine why hundreds of millions of people would submit themselves to a "devil" of a man, the Scriptures say it will happen. The coming tribulation will be like nothing the world has ever seen, so we must imagine the reality of people doing things to save themselves they might otherwise never have done. That includes submitting to a ruler who promises to deliver them from God's judgment.

A VERSE TO WRITE

"But you, go your way till the end; for you shall rest, and will arise to your inheritance at the end of the days."

DANIEL 12:13

REFLECT ON THIS

In Daniel 2:31–45, Nebuchadnezzar envisioned a colossal image of a man. Why do you think such an image appeared in his dream? What does it say about man's perspective on human achievements?

_____

_____

_____

_____

In Daniel 2:31–45, who is the stone? What part do today's Christians play in the growth of God's kingdom?

_____

_____

_____

_____

What is the greatest challenge you are facing? Read Daniel 6:1–13. How will you allow Daniel's prayer life to encourage you as you face this challenge?

_____

_____

_____

_____

GRACE AND MERCY

THE MINOR PROPHETS

~

"Return to Me, and I will return to you."

MALACHI 3:7

OFTEN OVERLOOKED, THE MINOR PROPHETS contain critical insights into God's relationship with His people. They illustrate God's enduring love and commitment to redeem those who call on His name.

Like us, the people of that day struggled to place God first in their lives. Even within the faith community, the rich marginalized the poor. Worship was hollow. The people postponed rebuilding the temple, God's dwelling place, to improve their own homes. Time and again, the Lord's work languished as the people pursued selfish desires.

Through all of this, the prophets portrayed God beckoning His people back. He met each act of rebellion with an invitation to redemption and restoration. When we understand how imperfectly the Old Testament believers followed God, we discover the depths of God's grace for our own failures. He does not hold our falls against us forever. There is a future after falling.

Grace provides something we don't deserve—forgiveness, a fresh start, and renewed hope. This forgiveness also involves mercy—not giving us the judgment and wrath we deserve. The past is over when it comes to the forgiveness of our sin. God's grace and mercy are indeed greater than all our sins.

No matter who you are or what you've done, God's grace buries your past and opens the door to a future of hope and blessing if you will receive His grace in your life today.

A VERSE TO WRITE

Then Haggai, the LORD's messenger, spoke the LORD's message to the people, saying, "I am with you, says the LORD."

HAGGAI 1:13

_____

_____

_____

_____

_____

_____

REFLECT ON THIS

How does Amos 5:21–23 compare to James 1:22–27 and Revelation 3:14–22?

_____

_____

_____

When Zephaniah prophesied, the people of Judah were "settled in complacency" (Zephaniah 1:12). Could this phrase be applied to your walk with the Lord? Why or why not? Ask the Lord to help you grow in humility and meekness, trusting in His strength rather than your own.

_____

_____

_____

Look up Nehemiah 1:9; Joel 2:13; Zechariah 1:3–4; and Malachi 3:7. What conditions did God give for returning to Him? What outcomes did He describe?

_____

_____

_____

A LOVE THAT NEVER ENDS

HOSEA

$\sim$

"I will betroth you to Me forever; yes, I will betroth you to Me in
righteousness and justice, in lovingkindness and mercy; I will betroth
you to Me in faithfulness, and you shall know the Lord."

HOSEA 2:19–20

HOSEA PROPHESIED TO THE TEN Northern tribes of
Israel just before they were carried into captivity by Assyria in 722
BC. It was a time of great prosperity but also of materialism and
idolatry. The theme of Hosea's prophecy was spiritual infidelity;
Israel had forsaken God for pagan idols.

Covenant is at the heart of marriage and the heart of our relationship with God—and loyalty is the fundamental characteristic of any
covenant. But after six hundred years of "marriage," Israel had forsaken God, so God sent Hosea to reveal the nation's adultery. Despite
this, Hosea's message affirmed God's loyal love for His covenant
people. Israel's spiritual adultery would not negate God's love.

To illustrate this message, God instructed Hosea to marry a

woman who would become unfaithful but to whom Hosea would remain loyal. So Hosea married Gomer, who was as disloyal to him as Israel was to God. But the prophecy didn't end there—Hosea anticipated a day when Israel's relationship with God would be healed and the "marriage" restored (2:16, 18–19).

If God stopped loving us, He would cease to be God because He is love (1 John 4:8, 16). God didn't stop loving Adam and Eve when they sinned, Noah when he got drunk, Abraham when he lied and doubted God, Moses when he disobeyed God, David when he committed adultery and was complicit in murder, Jonah when he ran away from God's assignment to preach in Nineveh, Peter when he denied knowing Christ, and the list goes on. God doesn't stop loving you when you sin either.

I don't mean to suggest that our sins are unimportant—they matter. And God may discipline us because of our sin, but that discipline flows from love, not anger or unforgiveness. The message of the Bible is clear from beginning to end: God loves you. He always has. He always will. And nowhere in Scripture is that truth more clearly illustrated than in the book of Hosea.

A VERSE TO WRITE

Come, and let us return to the LORD; for He has torn, but He will heal us; He has stricken, but He will bind us up.

HOSEA 6:1

REFLECT ON THIS

Read Hosea 11:1, 3–4. In what three ways does Hosea portray God's love?

_____

_____

_____

_____

With which portrayal of God's love do you most easily identify? Which one do you struggle with most? How does your study of Hosea deepen your understanding of God's love?

_____

_____

_____

_____

Read Obadiah 17. How do God's future blessings for Israel contrast with Israel's constant abandonment of God's law? What does this say about the loving mercy He extends to His people?

_____

_____

_____

_____

A MESSAGE FOR THE WORLD

JONAH

"Should I not pity Nineveh, that great city, in which are more than one hundred and twenty thousand persons who cannot discern between their right hand and their left—and much livestock?"

JONAH 4:11

DURING JEROBOAM II'S REIGN in the Northern Kingdom, Jonah's prophecies helped Israel expand its territory and influence (2 Kings 14:25). The prophet was well-known among his people and had direct access to the king. Naturally, he was reluctant to leave, especially when God's assignment involved a heavily fortified foreign city that was known for its barbaric cruelty.

Not only was Jonah afraid to visit the Ninevites; he also hated them. He would have preferred to see God's judgment fall than help them to escape it. His mindset illustrates three errors in thinking that can interfere with our ability to reach the lost.

STEREOTYPICAL. Jonah put every Assyrian into the same category: evil and unworthy of God's grace. Rather than seeing a composite of individuals, he saw their collective reputation. If we want to avoid similar attitudes, we need to walk among the people in our mission field to discover their uniqueness and identify those who are tender toward the truth of God's Word.

HISTORICAL. Jonah could not see past the Assyrians' cruelty. Their reputation was well earned, but he refused to imagine what they could become by the power of God's grace. Similarly, we need to ask God to help us envision how the gospel would transform people if His Word were released in their hearts.

HATEFUL. There was no denying the Assyrians' reputation and history of cruelty. They were sinful people. But because these factors shaped Jonah's perspective, he refused to have compassion for them. He compounded their wickedness with his own hatefulness. We might despise an ideology or an evil act, but we have a responsibility to separate the behavior from the perpetrator.

We will never escape God's presence or plan. His gifts and His call on our lives are irrevocable (Romans 11:29). Even if we cannot see His purpose, we can trust His direction in taking the gospel to the nations.

A VERSE TO WRITE

I know that You are a gracious and merciful God.

JONAH 4:2

_____

_____

_____

REFLECT ON THIS

What does Psalm 139:7–10 say about running from God's presence?

_____

_____

_____

_____

How does Jonah's calling demonstrate God's love for the nations? How does it foreshadow the Great Commission as seen in Matthew 28:16–20 and Mark 16:14–20?

_____

_____

_____

Read Jonah 4:11. Is there a people group you consider to be beyond God's reach? How will you commit them to His loving care?

_____

_____

_____

_____

_____

THE LORD IS OUR LIGHT

MICAH, NAHUM, AND HABAKKUK

~

*Though the fig tree may not blossom, nor fruit be on the vines; though
the labor of the olive may fail, and the fields yield no food; though the
flock may be cut off from the fold, and there be no herd in the stalls—yet
I will rejoice in the LORD, I will joy in the God of my salvation.*

HABAKKUK 3:17–18

WE WORSHIP WHOM WE TRUST, and we trust whom we
know. We come to this level of faith because we build trust, and we
build trust because we spend time with God.

Do you remember the experience of getting to know your best
friend—perhaps the person you married? You didn't initially fully
unburden your deepest thoughts because you didn't know whether
you could trust your new friend. Alas, there are lesser relationships
with people who fall by the wayside because they betray our trust
in some way. But your best friend was that person who redeemed
your trust, and you confirmed it only through the time and tears
of relationship.

The same principle holds true with God. You must come to know Him before you can really, truly, deeply trust Him. Then and only then will you be able to worship in spirit and in trust. Then and only then will you be able to say, in a twenty-first-century paraphrase of Habakkuk, "I may lose my work, my loved ones, and all that I own. Still I will love God all the more. Still I will praise Him with the loudest voice I can muster. And He will lift me up, for I know whom I have believed and am persuaded that He is able."

When we read and meditate on God's Word, we come to know Him more and more. To build the level of trust Habakkuk wrote about, we must start there. Through interacting with the Bible regularly, we come to trust God more and soon find ourselves at the place where we "rejoice in the LORD"!

A VERSE TO WRITE

Do not rejoice over me, my enemy; when I fall, I will arise;
when I sit in darkness, the LORD will be a light to me.

MICAH 7:8

_____

_____

_____

_____

_____

REFLECT ON THIS

Read Habakkuk 3:19. How is the Lord your strength?

_____

_____

_____

Read Micah 5:2. How is this verse fulfilled in the birth of Jesus? How would this verse have encouraged the people of Bethlehem when they heard it?

_____

_____

_____

In Nahum 1:7, Scripture says, "The LORD is good, a stronghold in the day of trouble; and He knows those who trust in Him." In what ways do you feel that God trusts in you? Can you earn that trust, or is it a gift?

_____

_____

_____

FEAR OF THE LORD IS THE
FOUNDATION OF TRUE
WISDOM. ALL WHO OBEY HIS
COMMANDMENTS WILL GROW IN
WISDOM. PRAISE HIM FOREVER!

PSALM 111:10 NLT

THE NEW TESTAMENT

Even before he made the world, God loved us and chose us
in Christ to be holy and without fault in his eyes.

EPHESIANS 1:4 NLT

WE ARE REDEEMED BY CHRIST

THE NEW TESTAMENT

⎯⎯⎯ ෴ ⎯⎯⎯

"For God so loved the world that He gave His only begotten Son, that whoever believes in Him should not perish but have everlasting life."

JOHN 3:16

AFTER THE LAST BOOK OF THE OLD TESTAMENT was written, Scripture fell silent for four hundred years. This period is called the Intertestamental Period. Alexander the Great defeated the Persians during this prolonged silence, and the Roman Empire began to expand, eventually claiming Judea and Jerusalem. Because of Rome's occupation, the Jews' longing for their promised Messiah intensified. He did not come as they expected, but when He came, His arrival changed world history forever.

The first four books of the New Testament are commonly called the Gospels because they relate to the life and ministry of Christ. In the book of Acts, we read how the early church took the gospel to other parts of the world. Later in the New Testament, the epistles teach us how the gospel impacts our daily life. They teach us how to love and serve God, live in harmony with one another, support the ministry of the church, and take the good news of Jesus around the world.

The Old and New Testaments are bound together by one recurring theme: redemption. This idea of being released from bondage is both the prevalent theme of God's Word and the reason why the Living Word, Jesus Christ, came to earth. Throughout the Old Testament, we find glimpses of God's redemptive plan. In the New Testament, we behold the redemptive work of Christ's death and resurrection in action—the Son of God becoming a man so that He might redeem us from our sin.

As believers, it is our high calling to share this good news with the lost and dying in our world today.

A VERSE TO WRITE

In Him we have redemption through His blood, the forgiveness of sins, according to the riches of His grace.

EPHESIANS 1:7

_____

_____

_____

_____

_____

REFLECT ON THIS

Read John 8:31–32 and 13:34–35. What are the marks of discipleship? On a scale of 1 to 10, how would you rate yourself in these areas?

_____

_____

_____

Read Ephesians 1:1–14. When did God choose us to be part of His family? List some of the blessings described in this passage that flow from that truth.

_____

_____

_____

Some people believe it's possible to please God by being a good person. Based on Romans 2:15, how would you answer them?

_____

_____

_____

DELIGHTING IN GOD'S WORD
LEADS US TO DELIGHT IN
GOD, AND DELIGHT IN GOD
DRIVES AWAY FEAR.

DAVID JEREMIAH

THE GOSPELS
AND ACTS

MATTHEW, MARK, LUKE, JOHN, AND ACTS

THE WORD *GOSPEL* MEANS "GOOD NEWS." When we share the gospel, we share the good news that Jesus is the Savior of the world and that new life is available through His life, death, and resurrection when we repent and trust in Him as our Savior and Lord.

The book of Acts is considered a historical book recounting the events of the Early Church. It is an extension of the gospel of Luke and is the result of Luke's scholarly research.

THE MESSIAH HAS ARRIVED

MATTHEW

"Who do men say that I, the Son of Man, am?" . . . Simon Peter answered
and said, "You are the Christ, the Son of the living God."

MATTHEW 16:13, 16

UNDER THE HOLY SPIRIT'S INSPIRATION, each of the
Gospels offers a unique presentation of the life of Christ. And
Matthew's account had one overriding purpose: to demonstrate
that the carpenter from Nazareth was the long-awaited Messiah—
Christ, the Anointed One. More than anything else that Jesus
said or did, His claim to be the Messiah incensed first-century
Jews. That is why Matthew began his book with a seventeen-verse,
forty-name genealogy, tracing Jesus' earthly lineage back some two
thousand years and forty-two generations.

This genealogy is as unique as the Person it represents. At the
time, a person's family tree established their status in society. People
would often omit undesirable names to improve their pedigree. But
Matthew's record of Jesus' genealogy includes a variety of surpris-
ing inclusions.

WOMEN. Matthew names five women as earthly ancestors of Jesus: Tamar, Rahab, Ruth, Bathsheba, and Mary. Including women was unheard of at the time, but it demonstrates Jesus' desire to break down the barrier between the sexes.

GENTILES. It gets worse. Three of the women in Jesus' genealogy weren't even Jews. Tamar, Rahab, and Ruth were from Canaan and Moab—nations detested by Israel.

SINNERS. Tamar tricked her father-in-law into having an incestuous relationship with her. Rahab was not only a Canaanite, but she was also a prostitute before joining the people of Israel. And if you recall the story of David and Bathsheba, you know that she committed adultery with David before he had her first husband killed.

What is the purpose of including such people in the Lord's genealogy? In the words of Tim Keller, "In Jesus Christ, prostitute and king, male and female, Jew and Gentile, one race and another race, moral and immoral—all sit down as equals. Equally sinful and lost, equally accepted and loved. In the old King James Bible, this chapter is filled with 'the begats'—'So and so begat so and so and so. . . .' Boring? No. The grace of God is so pervasive that even the begats of the Bible are dripping with God's mercy."[8]

A VERSE TO WRITE

She will bring forth a Son, and you shall call His name Jesus.

MATTHEW 1:21

REFLECT ON THIS

Based on Deuteronomy 23:3, why would it have shocked Matthew's original readers to see a Moabitess named in Jesus' genealogy?

_____

_____

_____

According to Matthew 1:19, 24, what spiritual virtues did Joseph possess?

_____

_____

_____

Jesus' virgin birth fulfilled a promise made more than six hundred years before He arrived in Bethlehem. Read Genesis 3:15, Isaiah 7:14, Isaiah 9:6–7, and Micah 5:2. How do these verses reveal that promise?

_____

_____

_____

THE WAY UP

MARK

"Whoever desires to become great among you shall be your servant. . . . For even the Son of Man did not come to be served, but to serve, and to give His life a ransom for many."

MARK 10:43, 45

MARK WAS THE SHORTEST AND THE FIRST of the four Gospels to be written. A sense of urgency marks his account—his favorite word being "immediately" (used thirty-six times). Solid extra-biblical evidence suggests that Mark wrote the Gospel in Rome during the last days of Peter's life, when persecution was breaking out against the church throughout the Roman Empire. Mark illuminates the urgency and seriousness of following Jesus as a disciple—in his day and ours.

Mark wasn't alone in his intensity. Jesus used His power to serve others with urgency and to sacrifice His life for the world. After He preached in Galilee, Jesus told His disciples, "Let us go into the next towns, that I may preach there also, because for this purpose I have come forth" (Mark 1:38).

According to Jesus, the Christian path to greatness comes through service and self-sacrifice. People are not on the receiving end of service but the giving end in the kingdom of God. In Acts 20:35, Paul reminded us of Jesus' words: "It is more blessed to give than to receive." Jesus took the whole issue of greatness and turned it on its head.

When James and John asked to sit beside Jesus in glory, He gave them a lesson in humility. He told them, "Whoever desires to become great among you shall be your servant. And whoever of you desires to be first shall be slave of all" (Mark 10:43–44).

The sad part of the story is that Jesus had spent months with these men, modeling servant leadership. But somehow, they had missed it all. Their request represented the attitude of the world when it comes to getting ahead. They wanted power and influence next to the throne. How disappointed Jesus must have been!

Greatness is all about serving. If you want to be great in the eyes of God, the way up is to get down on your knees before the Lord, serving Him.

A VERSE TO WRITE

"The Son of Man did not come to be served, but to serve."

MARK 10:45

REFLECT ON THIS

Read Mark 8:34–38. Following Jesus requires what three things?

_____

_____

_____

Read 1 John 3:16–23. How do we know that Jesus loves us? What is His ultimate commandment to us? How can we better live this out?

_____

_____

_____

In your own words, how are loving and serving others connected? How will you advance God's kingdom?

_____

_____

_____

NO ONE IS BEYOND JESUS' REACH

LUKE

"The Son of Man has come to seek and to save that which was lost."

LUKE 19:10

ACCORDING TO THE APOSTLE PAUL, Luke was a "beloved physician" (Colossians 4:14) who accompanied Paul on several missionary journeys. However, Luke's real passion was setting down an orderly account that detailed the birth, ministry, death, and resurrection of Jesus. As the Bible's only Gentile author, Luke emphasized Jesus' passion for saving the lost, especially those who imagine themselves to be "unredeemable."

Luke's Gospel contains thirty-five parables of Jesus; nineteen are unique to his book, including the Good Samaritan, the Lost Coin, and the Lost Son. They reveal great truths of love, grace, forgiveness, and the human element that captures our attention. These stories were not intended to entertain or to fill the pages of the Gospels. Jesus' word pictures were mighty weapons that He used to fill the minds of His hearers with truths they would never forget.

One parable that is unique to Luke's Gospel is the story of the two debtors, recorded in Luke 7:41–43. When Jesus pardoned the transgressions of the woman who washed His feet with her tears, He shared this parable to demonstrate His authority to forgive sins. Immediately after recounting the parable and the woman's forgiveness, Luke described a group of women "who had been healed of evil spirits and infirmities" (8:2), including Mary Magdalene.

Mary was called "Magdalene" because she was from the village of Magdala. Rife with prostitution, it had a reputation as an immoral place. The Gospel narrative of Mary Magdalene begins with reference to her former possession by seven demons. It ends a few years later when Jesus emerged from His tomb bearing the greatest news in history. The first person to receive the news wasn't Peter, John, or even Jesus' mother. It was Mary Magdalene. Of all the men and women then living in the world, the Lord chose her.

Luke's Gospel powerfully illustrates what Christ can do in a person's life.

A VERSE TO WRITE

"They will come from the east and the west, from the north and the south, and sit down in the kingdom of God."

LUKE 13:29

_____

_____

_____

REFLECT ON THIS

Read Luke 7:36–50. Why did Simon, the Pharisee host, doubt that Jesus was a prophet? How did Jesus' parable serve to address Simon's doubts?

_____

_____

_____

Read Luke 8:26–39. From the story of the demon-possessed man, what can you infer about Mary Magdalene's life before Jesus healed her?

_____

_____

_____

What is the most dramatic change that Jesus has brought about in your life?

_____

_____

_____

OUR PATH TO ETERNAL LIFE

JOHN

These are written that you may believe that Jesus is the Christ, the
Son of God, and that believing you may have life in His name.

JOHN 20:31

PUBLIC AND PERSONAL ENCOUNTERS with people from all walks of life punctuated Jesus' ministry. It is evident from the Gospels that He spent much of His time teaching people how to find salvation. Wherever Jesus went, He had one thing on His mind: to seek lost men and women and to bring them to a saving knowledge of God through faith. When John wrote his Gospel, Matthew, Mark, and Luke had already provided a comprehensive narrative of Jesus' life. Thus, John wrote his account to complement the others and, above all, to lead people to salvation in Christ.

Jesus had great insight into humanity's condition. In chapter 3, John related how a man named Nicodemus came seeking answers from Jesus. Nicodemus was a Pharisee, a wealthy member of the Sanhedrin—a ruler of the Jews—who lived in the highest level of religious life in his day. But he came to Jesus by night and said, "Rabbi, we know that You are a teacher come from God; for no one can do these signs that You do unless God is with him" (v. 2). In that statement, we see the searching heart of this religious leader.

Yet Nicodemus was wrong in his initial statement to Jesus. His theology wasn't correct because Jesus wasn't just a *teacher who came from God*—He was *God who came to teach*. Before the end of the conversation, Nicodemus would come to recognize that he wasn't simply dealing with a representative of God. Jesus Christ was God in a body—the Lord of glory.

As he closes his Gospel, John relates how the resurrected Christ comforted, prepared, encouraged, and restored His followers. He appeared to several disciples and breathed His Spirit into them to prepare them for ministry. When Thomas refused to believe in the resurrection, Jesus appeared to him and eased his doubts. Finally, Jesus restored fellowship with Peter after his three denials. John beautifully illustrates Jesus' heart for humanity.[9]

A VERSE TO WRITE

Jesus said to him, "I am the way, the truth, and the life. No one comes to the Father except through Me."

JOHN 14:6

REFLECT ON THIS

To whom was Jesus speaking when He spoke the words of John 3:16? What did Jesus tell him was necessary to obtain eternal life? (John 3:3–8, 15–16)

_____

_____

_____

Review John 21:15–17. What three commands did Jesus give to Peter?

_____

_____

_____

Jesus uplifted His disciples and instructed them to go out into the world and do the same for others. When you think of an uplifting person, what qualities come to mind? How can you incorporate those qualities into your own life?

_____

_____

_____

THE HOLY SPIRIT IGNITES THE EARLY CHURCH

ACTS

"You shall receive power when the Holy Spirit has come upon you; and you shall be witnesses to Me in Jerusalem, and in all Judea and Samaria, and to the end of the earth."

ACTS 1:8

FOLLOWING JESUS' DEATH, JERUSALEM was a dangerous place to be. Yet about 120 disciples remained in the upper room, waiting for "the Promise of the Father" and maintaining their unity in prayer as Jesus had instructed them to do (Acts 1:4, 14; 2:1). When the Promise arrived, it launched a movement that continues to this day.

Fifty days after Jesus' death, the sound of "a rushing mighty wind" from heaven suddenly filled the house where the disciples were gathered (Acts 2:2). It immediately alerted them that the promised Holy Spirit had arrived. It also would have captured the attention of any nearby pilgrims who were visiting Jerusalem for Pentecost.

At once, the Holy Spirit filled the disciples, symbolized by "tongues, as of fire" that sat upon each one (v. 3). Previously, they had believed in Christ, but they had not been baptized by the Holy Spirit because Christ had not ascended into heaven. After He did, the Holy Spirit came down to dwell in the church—that group of people who had identified themselves with Jesus. In their day (and in ours), the Spirit's baptism binds believers together and establishes an invisible union among them.

To further jump-start the church, the Holy Spirit empowered all 120 disciples "to speak with other tongues" (v. 4). This supernatural speech was not unintelligible, ecstatic utterances. It was human speech, uttered in known human languages by people who had no facility in those languages before the Spirit gave them utterance. According to verse 6, pilgrims from every nation "heard them speak in his own language."

When the Pentecost crowds returned to their homes, they kept the memory of this miracle. And no doubt, many were part of the three thousand saved when Peter preached the gospel. This miracle of speaking in other tongues allowed the gospel to spread throughout the Mediterranean and Middle Eastern world.

A VERSE TO WRITE

You shall receive the gift of the Holy Spirit.

ACTS 2:38

_____

_____

REFLECT ON THIS

Review Acts 1:9–11. Who witnessed this event? Why do you think the Holy Spirit commanded them to wait together in Jerusalem?

_____

_____

_____

Read John 14:16, 19; Acts 2:1–21; Ephesians 5:18. How would you describe the work of the Holy Spirit in the believer's life?

_____

_____

_____

Read Acts 2:42–47 and 4:32–37. How can you contribute to the health of your local church?

_____

_____

_____

THE SCRIPTURES SHOW US
SO CLEARLY THAT NOTHING
IN LIFE IS WASTED IF WE
LOVE AND SERVE GOD.

DR. DAVID JEREMIAH

THE EPISTLES

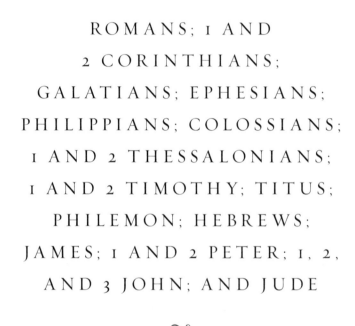

ROMANS; 1 AND
2 CORINTHIANS;
GALATIANS; EPHESIANS;
PHILIPPIANS; COLOSSIANS;
1 AND 2 THESSALONIANS;
1 AND 2 TIMOTHY; TITUS;
PHILEMON; HEBREWS;
JAMES; 1 AND 2 PETER; 1, 2,
AND 3 JOHN; AND JUDE

THERE ARE TWENTY-ONE INSTRUCTIONAL letters in the New Testament addressed to believers in developing churches. Written by the leaders of the early church, these books guide churches through doctrinal issues, worship practices, and other Christian teachings that continue to impact followers today.

GIFTS FOR BELIEVERS

ROMANS

⁓

*I am not ashamed of the gospel of Christ, for it is the power
of God to salvation for everyone who believes.*

ROMANS 1:16

MANY SCHOLARS REGARD ROMANS as the greatest of
Paul's letters and one of the foundational documents of Christianity.
Paul addressed various topics, but all point to the truth that a loving God has offered salvation to sinful humanity through the death
and resurrection of His Son.

In chapter 6, Paul taught that God's purpose for us reaches
beyond our initial response to His offer of grace and forgiveness.
God wants us to become, in practice, what we have already become
in position. As Paul unfolded this truth of sanctification, he gave us
three keys to victorious living.

KNOW (ROMANS 6:8-10). With many churches pushing
doctrine into the shadows, it is compelling to observe the signifi-
cance Paul placed on "knowing." We need to *know* that Christ died

to take away our sin, which means believers also died to the penalty and power of sin. Because of our shared death and resurrection, we *know* that we are free from sin.

RECKON (ROMANS 6:11). Appearing nineteen times, the word *reckon* ("consider," "regard," "look upon," or "count," depending on the translation) is a crucial word in Romans. The Greek word *logizomai* has to do with the reality of the way things are. It acknowledges something that is already true. Paul told us, as Christians, to reckon, conclude, and accept that we are no longer slaves to sin but have been set free.

YIELD (ROMANS 6:12-14). "Therefore" is significant at the beginning of verse 12. It tells us that because of what we have learned about our identification with Christ in His death, burial, and resurrection—because we have died to the reign of sin and death and have come alive in grace and life—we should not allow sin to control us. Instead, Paul called us to yield ourselves entirely to Christ and His righteousness (verses 13–14).

Reading Romans often feels like being swept along in a rapid, but it leads us to the conclusion that we serve a merciful God who faithfully fulfills His plans for us. His freedom, grace, and power are available to all who believe!

A VERSE TO WRITE

If we died with Christ, we believe that we shall also live with Him.

ROMANS 6:8

REFLECT ON THIS

Read 1 Corinthians 8:9; Galatians 5:1; 1 Peter 2:15–16; and James 1:25. What do these passages reveal about the freedom that is ours in Christ?

_____

_____

_____

Study Romans 1:16–17; and 6:1–23. Who is responsible for the work of justification in our life? What about sanctification?

_____

_____

_____

What would you say to someone who claims that God's forgiveness and grace give us the freedom to do whatever we want?

_____

_____

_____

STAYING FAITHFUL TO GOD'S CALL

1 AND 2 CORINTHIANS

My speech and my preaching were . . . in demonstration of the Spirit and of power,
that your faith should not be in the wisdom of men but in the power of God.

1 CORINTHIANS 2:4–5

"MY GRACE IS SUFFICIENT FOR YOU, for My strength is made perfect in weakness" (2 Corinthians 12:9). This statement by our Lord is one of the most beloved sentiments in Scripture, yet we often overlook its context. It appears toward the end of Paul's second letter to Corinth, and it is the centerpiece of his defense against false teachers who were challenging his authority. Why should believers accept his teaching? Among other reasons, Paul argued that they should listen to him because God's power was evident in his life.

We demonstrate our integrity when we stick with our commitments without wavering, even when grueling times arrive. Paul emphasized this quality in his teaching. He told the Romans that perseverance creates hopeful hearts (Romans 5:3–5). Paul instructed the Ephesians to be "watchful to this end with all perseverance and supplication for all the saints" (Ephesians 6:18). He reminded Timothy, "But you have carefully followed my doctrine, manner of life, purpose, faith, longsuffering, love, perseverance" (2 Timothy 3:10). And in 2 Corinthians 12:12, he told the Corinthians about his perseverance as he labored among them and faced significant opposition.

Paul had learned that spiritual strength does not come through natural human ability but through Christ. In one of the most honest expressions in all of Scripture, he admitted that God caused him to have "a thorn in the flesh" (2 Corinthians 12:7) to keep his pride in check. By becoming weak in his circumstances, Paul developed a deeper dependence on God.

Paul wasn't trying to impress anyone. When those in Corinth criticized him, he just stayed faithful to what God had called him to do, focusing on the grace and power of Christ in him rather than on any strengths or shortcomings of his own. Through Paul's testimony of personal weakness, we understand that serving in God's kingdom begins with seeing our limitations.

A VERSE TO WRITE

And He said to me, "My grace is sufficient for you, for My strength is made perfect in weakness."
2 CORINTHIANS 12:9

_____

_____

_____

REFLECT ON THIS

According to Acts 9:13–14, 21, why was there so much skepticism about Paul being an apostle? How did Paul view his suitability to represent the Lord, as seen in Acts 22:3–5 and 26:9–11?

_____

_____

_____

Read Acts 20:1–38; 1 Corinthians 3:3; and 13:5. What does this tell you about the attributes of authentic spiritual leaders?

_____

_____

_____

Why is it just as wrong to underestimate ourselves as it is to overestimate ourselves? What danger goes along with each error?

_____

_____

_____

CHRIST IS ENOUGH

GALATIANS

❧

Stand fast therefore in the liberty by which Christ has made us free,
and do not be entangled again with a yoke of bondage.

GALATIANS 5:1

SINCE THE BEGINNING OF CHRISTIANITY, people have tried to change the gospel. Some have described it in terms of doing good works, while others emphasize avoidance of sinful behaviors. But the gospel is simply this: the good news that Christ came and died for our sins so that we might become God's children. Paul's letter to the Galatians is a magnificent defense of the gospel of grace.

Believers in Galatia were feeling pressure to add works to their salvation. Instead of focusing on Christ and all that He is, they had allowed someone to take them backward in their faith. In response, Paul wrote a passionate exploration of grace versus the law that is every bit as compelling as Victor Hugo's *Les Misérables*.

In Galatians 3:1–5, Paul contrasted the law with grace by asking five questions. First, he asked about the Person of Christianity and challenged the impossibility of salvation through legalism. He reasoned that if the Galatians had kept their gaze fixed on Christ, they would have been immune to false doctrine.

Paul's second question pertained to the process of salvation. When the Galatians accepted Christ, they received the Holy Spirit without earning God's favor. It was—and is—a gift. The Holy Spirit is the believer's most unmistakable proof of salvation and the surest guarantee of eternal glory (Romans 8:16).

Third, he asked about Christian perfection, or maturity, which also comes through faith in Christ Jesus. There is not one thing a Christian can do to gain God's acceptance. Paul's fourth question implied that it was hard for him to believe that the Galatians would abandon their faith after overcoming persecution.

Finally, Paul inquired about the power of Christianity. He wanted the Galatians to remember that the gift of the Holy Spirit and His mighty work was solely dependent on their faith in Christ.

Paul's questions point to the supernatural. Christianity can only be explained in terms of God! His Son died for us and gave His life for us. Now He freely offers us salvation, allowing us to approach God by faith.

A VERSE TO WRITE

You are all sons of God through faith in Christ Jesus.

GALATIANS 3:26

_____

_____

_____

REFLECT ON THIS

Read Galatians 2:16. In what ways has legalism crept into your thinking?

_____

_____

_____

According to Galatians 5:22–26, what causes spiritual fruit to grow in a believer's life?

_____

_____

_____

Spend some time in prayer, thanking the Lord that Christ is enough and asking Him to help you maintain a healthy perspective of your freedom in Christ.

_____

_____

_____

LIVING IN THE SPIRIT

EPHESIANS

I pray that from his glorious, unlimited resources he [the Father]
will empower you with inner strength through his Spirit.
EPHESIANS 3:16 NLT

WHEN WE ACCEPT JESUS CHRIST as our Savior, the Holy
Spirit lives within us, or "indwells" us. He also brings us into the
body of Christ, which is called the "baptism of the Spirit." But
when the Spirit comes to live within us, He does not always get
control of us. Paul's letter to the Ephesians helps us see how living
with a sense of victory requires yielding control to the Holy Spirit.

Ephesians 5:18 *commands* us to be filled with the Holy Spirit.
This is a continuous process whereby we give the Lord control over
our lives. There are four conditions for being filled with the Spirit.

DESIRE TO BE FILLED WITH THE SPIRIT. Matthew
5:6 says that blessing comes when we "hunger and thirst for righteousness." Many believers attend church, but they never move
ahead with God. They hold back because they are afraid that He

might lead them somewhere they don't care to go. The way to move forward is to develop a holy hunger for the things of God.

DENOUNCE SIN. The Holy Spirit cannot fill us while we are harboring sin. We must denounce it, confess it, and forsake it. If we allow sin to remain in our life, the Holy Spirit will not take control.

DEDICATE OURSELVES FULLY TO CHRIST. To be filled with the Spirit is to be yielded to His control. God loves us and knows us better than anyone else. He can accomplish great things in us. But we limit the Spirit's power in our life when we do not follow His direction.

DEPEND DAILY ON THE SPIRIT. What does it mean to walk in the Spirit? It means putting one foot in front of the other, trusting the Lord in every moment. Galatians 5:16 says, "Walk in the Spirit, and you shall not fulfill the lust of the flesh."

The Spirit-filled believer will have the most thrilling life of anybody on earth. But it requires stepping out in faith and walking into the Lord's open arms. He is ready. Are you?

A VERSE TO WRITE

There is one body and one Spirit, just as you were called in one hope of your calling.
EPHESIANS 4:4

_____

_____

_____

REFLECT ON THIS

Read Matthew 3:11; Luke 11:13; John 14:26; Acts 1:8; 2:4, 38; 4:31; Romans 8; 1 Corinthians 6:18–20; 12:13; and Galatians 5:22. What do these verses reveal about the Holy Spirit?

> God is the author of the Bible, and only the truth it contains will lead people to true happiness.
> GEORGE MÜLLER

_____

_____

_____

_____

Read Ephesians 4:25–32 and 1 Thessalonians 5:19–20. According to these verses, what activities hinder the Holy Spirit's activity in our life?

_____

_____

_____

Read Ephesians 6:10–20. What is the connection between being filled with the Holy Spirit and spiritual warfare?

_____

_____

_____

WEARING JOY-TINTED GLASSES

PHILIPPIANS

*Let your conduct be worthy of the gospel of Christ. . . . For to you it has been granted
on behalf of Christ, not only to believe in Him, but also to suffer for His sake.*

PHILIPPIANS 1:27, 29

WHEN PAUL BEGAN PREACHING in Philippi in Acts 16, he
attracted both converts and critics. The critics seized him, stripped
him, and whipped him until blood ran down his back. But to Paul,
the church was worth the beating. It was to these beloved people
that Paul revealed his greatest desires—his regrets, successes, failures, passions, plans, and determination. By studying his letter to
the Philippians, we can sharpen our focus and find joy, no matter
our circumstances.

FOCUS ON GOD'S PURPOSE. Although God has an
individual plan for each of our lives, His ultimate purpose is to
transform us into the image of His Son, Jesus Christ. Spiritual
success comes by allowing Jesus to live His life through us by the
Holy Spirit.

FOCUS ON GOD'S PERSPECTIVE. In Philippians 3:13, Paul talks about "forgetting" the past and "reaching forward" to what's ahead. This includes our successes and failures. While history lends perspective for the future, lingering in the past for too long can allow our recollections to obliterate our dreams. By concentrating on God's grace and the power of Christ's resurrection, we can meet the future with fresh enthusiasm.

FOCUS ON GOD'S PLAN. The Lord has a distinct blueprint for our lives. It is tailor-designed for the way He made each of us and the experiences we've had. Everything leading up to today has prepared us for what's next. But we must follow Him into an unknown future.

FOCUS ON GOD'S PRIZE. When viewed from the perspective of eternity, life's troubles take on a different priority. By fixing our thoughts on heaven, we gain new motivation to "fight the good fight of faith" with gladness (1 Timothy 6:12).

At the core of Paul's life was one motivating principle: no matter what happened, he trusted the Lord's plan for his life. Let's adopt Paul's attitude, take up his torch, and serve the Lord with passion and joy.

A VERSE TO WRITE

Rejoice in the Lord always. Again I will say, rejoice!

PHILIPPIANS 4:4

_____

_____

REFLECT ON THIS

What do Romans 8:29; 2 Corinthians 3:18; and 1 Timothy 1:15 say about God's purpose for us?

_____

_____

_____

Read Matthew 25:21; 1 Corinthians 2:9; 2 Timothy 4:8; and 1 Peter 5:4. What do these verses say about the rewards that await us in heaven?

_____

_____

_____

Who needs your encouragement this week? How will you commit to staying positive, confident, hopeful, and encouraged in the Lord?

_____

_____

_____

JESUS IS OUR LORD

COLOSSIANS

See to it that no one takes you captive by philosophy and empty deceit, according to human tradition, according to the elemental spirits of the world, and not according to Christ.

COLOSSIANS 2:8 ESV

DURING PAUL'S FIRST IMPRISONMENT in Rome, false teachers infiltrated the Colossian church. Unable to visit, he penned a response that proclaimed Jesus Christ's lordship and sufficiency to meet our needs. By affirming authentic biblical doctrine, Paul's letter has equipped generations of believers to detect heresy. It also reminds us that disruptive events don't have to distract us; they can redirect our passion toward God's eternal purposes. Consider these truths from Colossians 3.

OUR IDENTITY IN CHRIST. Verses 1–4 say, "If then you were raised with Christ. . . . Your life is hidden with Christ. . . . You also will appear with Him in glory." Christ did not die on our behalf; He died in our place. We were crucified with Christ. Our old self is dead; our new self is alive and victorious in Christ.

OUR AUTHORITY WITH CHRIST. What image comes to your mind when you think of Jesus? Do you envision Him as lowly, meek, and mild (Matthew 11:29) or as the Lion of Judah? Mental images make a difference. The reality is that Jesus is risen, seated at the right hand of the Father; and when we see Him again, He will appear in all His magnificence. When we focus on His power and authority, our faith surges, and the allure of substitutes fades.

OUR SECURITY WITH CHRIST. Colossians 3:3 says, "For you died, and your life is hidden with Christ in God." Part of the meaning of "hidden with Christ" is that our identity and purpose in life are hidden from those who are outside of Christ. They don't understand us, but we have the knowledge that in Christ, we are secure.

OUR DESTINY WITH CHRIST. Part of being with Christ is becoming more like Him. When He appears at the end of this age, "then [we] also will appear with Him in glory" (Colossians 3:4). When He returns in glory, the change will be sudden and dramatic. All who have called Him Savior will be fully renewed—in spirit, mind, and body.

A VERSE TO WRITE

He is the image of the invisible God, the firstborn over all creation.

COLOSSIANS 1:15

REFLECT ON THIS

Read Romans 6:4–5; Galatians 2:20; Ephesians 2:6; and Colossians 3:1. What do these verses say about our identity in Christ?

_____

_____

_____

What are some ways that people try to earn salvation today? What scripture could you share with them?

_____

_____

_____

Read Galatians 5:1. Ask God to reveal any tendencies toward legalism that might be detracting from the freedom that is yours in Christ.

_____

_____

_____

_____

HAVING FAITH WHEN YOU'RE STRUGGLING

1 AND 2 THESSALONIANS

———— ∾ ————

We also pray . . . that our God would count you worthy of this calling, and fulfill
all the good pleasure of His goodness and the work of faith with power, that the
name of our Lord Jesus Christ may be glorified in you, and you in Him.

2 THESSALONIANS 1:11–12

JESUS ASSURED HIS DISCIPLES that He would return for them. But as the church in Thessalonica faced persecution, many converts wondered whether the end times had already begun. In response, Paul wrote two letters. The first letter instructed them in the truth, and the second corrected some errors that had occurred in the church. He also offered encouragement through praise, perspective, and prayer.

Every aspect of Paul's reassurance can strengthen believers today. But for this week's study, let's examine Paul's prayers for the Thessalonian believers. They offer three precepts for any believer facing trials—to be found worthy, fruitful, and faithful.

WORTHY. Trials do not *make* us what we are. Instead, they reveal what we already are. Notice that Paul did not pray for God to remove the Thessalonians' problems. Instead, he prayed that God would look inside their hearts and find a faith that would endure trials in His name. Those worthy to suffer for Him are those whose faith remains strong and committed when troubles come.

FRUITFUL. Fulfilling "all the good pleasure of His goodness and the work of faith with power" refers to the outgrowth of trials in a believer's life. Sometimes when trouble comes, we are tempted to retreat and hope the problem goes away. But we do not have to yield to that temptation. Like the early church, we can grow by serving God during difficult circumstances.

FAITHFUL. Paul's final prayer for the Thessalonians is that God would grant them such grace that their lives would glorify Jesus Christ. Trials can sharpen our faith by bringing the future into focus as we anticipate the victory and vindication that will come with Christ's return. When we suffer, we gain empathy and love for others who suffer. As God's people, the way we respond to hard times reflects our faith.

A VERSE TO WRITE

The Lord Himself will descend from heaven with a shout, with the voice of an archangel, and with the trumpet of God.

1 THESSALONIANS 4:16

REFLECT ON THIS

Read 2 Thessalonians 1:1–5. What reasons does Paul give for praising the Thessalonians?

_____

_____

_____

What perspective does Paul offer in 2 Thessalonians 1:6–10?

_____

_____

Looking back on your own experiences with trials and suffering, what have they revealed about your faith? What benefits have they brought?

_____

_____

_____

Read 1 Thessalonians 1:6–10. During these difficult circumstances why do you think Paul reminded the people of how they first came to follow Christ? Have you ever been tempted to turn away from your faith because of trials and suffering in your life?

_____

_____

THE NEXT GENERATION

1 AND 2 TIMOTHY

Preach the word! Be ready in season and out of season. Convince,
rebuke, exhort, with all longsuffering and teaching.

2 TIMOTHY 4:2

THE FIRST CENTURY WAS A CHALLENGING time to
establish Christ's church. When Paul wrote to Timothy, his time
was running out. Imprisoned twelve feet underground, Paul penned
a final letter to his young protégé. He charged Timothy to fight the
good fight, finish the race, and keep the faith. He knew the truth
of God's Word would anchor the church. Two thousand years later,
we also live in chaotic times, but 2 Timothy 4:2 teaches us how to
remain confident in the Word.

In an uncertain world like ours, we need God's Word. Paul
commanded Timothy, "Preach the word!" The word *preach* in the
New Testament means "to proclaim publicly, officially; to stand in
the marketplace and declare your message." With his own life coming to an end, Paul knew that young leaders like Timothy would

bear the responsibility for keeping the faith alive, and they would need to be bold. When everything around us is changing, we can cling to the truth that has been settled from eternity past in the mind of God.

"Be ready in season and out of season" conveys a sense of urgency. God's Word can make the difference between life and death to those who hear. Whether or not we are preachers by vocation, we will do well to apply Scripture to the times in which we live.

These three words, "convince, rebuke, exhort," relate to the needs of those who hear the Word preached. To change someone's mind requires convincing evidence, challenging their assumptions about sin, and offering encouragement toward the right path. Regular exposure to God's Word will convince the mind, convict the will, and comfort the heart.

Finally, Paul instructed Timothy to preach "with all longsuffering and teaching." That is, his teaching and preaching were to be sensitive. A change of heart usually takes time. When we present the gospel, we are to be patient as we faithfully declare "the whole counsel of God" (Acts 20:27), trusting that the Holy Spirit will awaken the mind.

A VERSE TO WRITE

Let no one despise your youth, but be an example to the believers.

1 TIMOTHY 4:12

_____

_____

REFLECT ON THIS

According to 2 Timothy 4:3–4, why is preaching the Word so important? Do you see any correlating signs in our culture?

_____

_____

_____

Read Psalm 119:89; Romans 12:2; 1 Thessalonians 4:18; and Hebrews 4:12. What do these verses say about the power of Scripture?

_____

_____

_____

Read 2 Timothy 1:6–11. With whom could you share your faith this week?

_____

_____

_____

Read 1 Timothy 6:11–12. What are some things you need to flee from in order to "lay hold on eternal life"? What godly attitudes will be needed to flee these sinful things?

_____

_____

GOD'S PEOPLE

TITUS

The grace of God that brings salvation has appeared to all men, teaching
us that, denying ungodliness and worldly lusts, we should live soberly,
righteously, and godly in the present age . . . zealous for good works.

TITUS 2:11–12, 14

IN PAUL'S LETTER TO TITUS, he emphasized the role of God's grace in His plan of redemption as he charged the young pastor with planting churches in a place known for its "liars, evil beasts," and "lazy gluttons" (1:12). Titus 2:11–14 outlines five ways God's grace enables Christians of any era to live victoriously over sin.

GRACE TEACHES US TO RENOUNCE SIN. When the Holy Spirit lives in us, He warns us anytime we are in danger of plunging into sin. We find ourselves unable to tolerate sin in our heart. By God's grace, we gain the power to renounce evil in all its forms.

GRACE TEACHES US TO GOVERN OURSELVES. Once we realize the extent of Christ's suffering for us, grace overwhelms us with a sense of God's holiness—and the price Christ paid for our salvation. It motivates us to live "soberly, righteously, and godly" (2:12). Instead of living for ourselves, we look for ways to express our gratitude to God by bringing Him glory.

GRACE TEACHES US TO RESPECT OTHERS. Living "righteously" has to do with how we treat other people. Considering the number of split churches throughout the centuries, the church of Jesus Christ has not always done this well. Yet the way we treat people for whom Christ died reflects our attitude toward Christ Himself.

GRACE TEACHES US TO REVERENCE GOD. Reverencing God simply means living a godly life that manifests Christlike qualities and characteristics. How do we become godly? Spending time in the Bible and practicing spiritual disciplines like prayer and worship will cause us to bear spiritual fruit.

GRACE TEACHES US TO RESIST LAZINESS. While good works are powerless to save us, Ephesians 2:10 says we were saved "for good works." There is kingdom work to be done in this world, and those rescued by grace carry it out.

When we encounter difficult people, it can be easy to forget how sinful we were before receiving the Holy Spirit. But like those difficult people, we needed God's grace to free us from sin's power.

A VERSE TO WRITE

Be peaceable, gentle, showing all humility to all.

TITUS 3:3

REFLECT ON THIS

Read Ephesians 2. What reasons do you find for being gracious toward difficult people?

_____

_____

_____

Read Psalm 5:12; 2 Corinthians 5:21; Colossians 3:5–10; James 1:22–27; and 1 John 1:9. What do these verses say about righteous living?

_____

_____

_____

What can you do to live in grace instead of being trapped by unforgiveness?

_____

_____

_____

_____

FREE TO FORGIVE

PHILEMON

I appeal to you for my son Onesimus, whom I have begotten while in my chains.
PHILEMON 10

PAUL WROTE MOST OF HIS LETTERS to church leaders who would share them publicly. But not so with the little book of Philemon. As the only private letter in the New Testament, it contains Paul's impassioned plea to a slaveholder on behalf of a runaway slave. It is deeply personal, yet it illustrates the universal, unifying message of the gospel.

While he was on the run, Onesimus (the slave) met Paul in Rome and became a believer. Onesimus gained freedom from the bonds of sin, but he was still bound by Rome's laws, which allowed for his execution as a runaway. Although Paul yearned to keep his "beloved brother" (v. 16) with him, he knew that Onesimus could not be truly free until he made amends with his slaveholder, Philemon. It was a difficult decision, but Paul sent Onesimus back to Philemon.

We discover several clues about Philemon from Paul's letter. Paul greeted him as a "beloved friend and fellow laborer" (v. 1). This description tells us that Philemon knew Paul, that they were good friends, and that Philemon was a believer. Later in the letter, Paul indicated that he led Philemon to Christ, trusted Philemon to pray for his release, and had plans to visit Philemon (vv. 19, 22). From this position of unity and brotherly love, Paul appealed to Philemon as a fellow worker and a faithful friend.

Some may wonder why Paul didn't rail against the institution of slavery. It's impossible for us to see the world through his eyes, but we know that slavery was woven into the fabric of Roman society, with some sixty million people in bondage. And remember, Christians were a persecuted minority. While the rebellion of a few could not upend slavery, Paul could reach every level of society from the inside out by introducing love into the hearts of both slaves and masters.

The gospel we proclaim binds us together. Romans 6:6 says, "Our old man was crucified with Him, that . . . we should no longer be slaves of sin." We all need God's forgiveness, and we all will receive it—if only we will return to our Master and ask.

A VERSE TO WRITE

No longer as a slave but more than a slave—a beloved brother, especially to me but how much more to you, both in the flesh and in the Lord.

PHILEMON 16

REFLECT ON THIS

What do the following verses say about God's forgiveness? Psalm 32:5; 103:10–14; Luke 7:44–50; Acts 2:38; 3:19; and 1 John 1:9–10; 2:1

_____

_____

_____

_____

Read Matthew 6:14–15; 18:21–22; Mark 11:25; Luke 6:37; 17:3–4; and Ephesians 4:32. What do these verses say about forgiving others?

_____

_____

_____

Onesimus left Philemon as a slave and returned as a brother in Christ. By forgiving him and granting him freedom, Philemon participated in God's plan for Onesimus's life. Is there someone you need to forgive? Or do you need to seek forgiveness from someone you've wronged?

_____

_____

_____

_____

A LOVING FATHER

HEBREWS

~

Let us therefore come boldly to the throne of grace, that we may
obtain mercy and find grace to help in time of need.

HEBREWS 4:16

THE LETTER TO THE HEBREWS was addressed primarily to Jewish people who had converted to Christianity. Facing opposition, some converts had reverted to Judaism or incorporated some of its elements into their faith. It is somewhat understandable; most of us go through life trying to avoid pain. But Hebrews teaches the opposite. While we aren't to seek out trouble, we can look for hidden lessons and blessings when trouble finds us.

According to Hebrews 12:7–8, God uses trials to correct us and prove our sonship. As our Father, He will always be there when we need Him. Difficulties allow us to call out to Him and confirm His presence.

It would be less than honest to suggest that trials are anything but painful. The writer of Hebrews used these words: "Chastening . . . rebuked . . . scourges. . . . Corrected. . . . Painful" (12:5–6, 9, 11). Children don't wish for their fathers to discipline them, because it hurts. Yet there is a divine purpose in times of correction and training.

Are you ready for some lighthearted news? "God deals with you as with sons" (Hebrews 12:7). The *pain* that causes us to question God's love is the *proof* of God's love! Punishment is a penalty for sin, but discipline is the training a loving father gives his children. When we walk through painful circumstances, our Father is never far from us.

Everything that happens to us, every struggle, is an opportunity. When trials come, we can rail against God, we can hang our heads and quit, or we can trust Him to use them for our benefit. He wants us to "be partakers of His holiness" and to yield "the peaceable fruit of righteousness" (Hebrews 12:10–11). Some lessons cannot be learned any other way.

The crucible of adversity shapes our character and substance. The right question is never, "Why, Lord?" It is always, "What, Lord? What do You want to teach me?" By responding this way, we gain greater access to His power, righteousness, and fruit.

A VERSE TO WRITE

For whom the LORD loves He chastens.

HEBREWS 12:6

REFLECT ON THIS

Read John 15:1–8. How do painful circumstances make us more fruitful?

_____

_____

_____

_____

Read Hebrews 4:15 and 5:7–10. What can we learn from Christ's response to suffering?

_____

_____

_____

Can you think of a time when God used trials to refine you spiritually? What did you learn through that experience?

_____

_____

_____

TRUE FAITH

JAMES

*What does it profit, my brethren, if someone says he has faith but does not have
works? Can faith save him? ... Faith by itself, if it does not have works, is dead.*
JAMES 2:14, 17

WHEN JAMES WROTE HIS LETTER, some individuals
spoke the language of Christianity without reflecting the reality
of its truth in their lives. Two thousand years later, not much has
changed. People still want to call themselves Christians without
conforming to its teachings. James 2:14–26 is one of the most con-
troversial texts in the New Testament because it highlights several
reasons why true faith requires more than a verbal affirmation.

Verse 14 poses two rhetorical questions to illustrate the insin-
cerity of a faith that does not demonstrate itself in works. Now,
James did not say that salvation hinges on our efforts. The whole
Bible is opposed to that. Paul reasoned that if we have been born
anew, the old things will pass away, and all things will become new
(2 Corinthians 5:17). Our life will be the proof.

In verses 15–16, James illustrates the futility of a words-only
profession of faith: imagine a person showing up at the door of a

believer to ask for help, but instead of helping the needy person, the Christian says, "Depart in peace, be warm and filled"—without giving him the things he needs. We commonly do that by saying a prayer instead of offering aid to someone with a real, tangible need. According to James, that casts doubt upon the integrity of our faith. Rather than asking God to help these people, we can help them! That is why He sent them to us in the first place. If our day-to-day lifestyle does not reflect our beliefs, our faith may not be genuine.

James makes a strong summary statement in verse 17: faith without works "is dead." In other words, it was never alive, and the lack of fruit is proof of a words-only faith. In Matthew 7:21, Jesus affirms this claim: "Not everyone who says to Me, 'Lord, Lord,' shall enter the kingdom of heaven, but he who does the will of My Father in heaven."

Christianity is a dynamic, powerful force in our lives. Genuine faith produces good works.

A VERSE TO WRITE

Be doers of the word, and not hearers only, deceiving yourselves.
JAMES 1:22

_____

_____

_____

_____

REFLECT ON THIS

Read 1 John 3:17–18. How does this passage compare to James 2:15–16? What does it say about loving others?

_____

_____

_____

Read Ephesians 2:8–10. According to this passage, what is the basis of our salvation? Why did God create us?

_____

_____

_____

In your own words, how would you explain the relationship between grace and works?

_____

_____

_____

WE ARE JUST PASSING THROUGH

1 AND 2 PETER

Sanctify the Lord God in your hearts, and always be ready to give a defense
to everyone who asks you a reason for the hope that is in you.

1 PETER 3:15

ONE OF PETER'S THEMES is the idea of being a traveler passing through life on the way to heaven (1 Peter 2:11). When we realize this world is not our home, it changes our approach to everything. Our possessions won't last; only what we send ahead of us will endure as we invest in God's kingdom. With this view of our Christian identity, how do we live it out?

LIVE LIKE WE BELONG. In a fractured world, the gospel of Jesus Christ offers the ultimate assurance that we belong. When we come to Jesus Christ, our sense of identity is bound up in Him. Regardless of race, gender, background, citizenship, political party, or social or financial status, we are His special people. Nothing in the world anchors our sense of belonging more deeply than claiming our identity in Christ and following His clear instructions for our life.

KEEP OUR EYES ON HEAVEN. When we keep the destination in mind, the trip is worth it. Heaven is sinless, pure, perfect, beautiful, and radiant. The closer we get to heaven, the more we should reflect its character. While we can't fully imagine how wonderful it will be, the Bible's descriptions allow our mind's eye to visualize heaven's city, walls, streets, golden glow, crystal river, God's throne, and the worshiping throngs. In Colossians 3, Paul tells us to keep our heart and mind focused on the things above.

CARRY OUT OUR ASSIGNMENT. As the Lord's stewards, we represent Him. A steward is someone who faithfully carries out the wishes of an owner, acting on his behalf, doing what he knows the owner would do in any situation. Our assignment is to glorify God through our words, thoughts, and actions wherever possible. It requires putting Jesus first and letting Him be Lord over everything in our life.

The world is full of people who need Christ's gift of salvation. They need a godly person to show them the way. Why not let it be us?

A VERSE TO WRITE

Rejoice to the extent that you partake of Christ's sufferings, that when His glory is revealed, you may also be glad with exceeding joy.

1 PETER 4:13

_____

_____

_____

REFLECT ON THIS

Read Genesis 47:9; 1 Chronicles 29:15; Psalm 84:5; Hebrews 11:13; and 1 Peter 1:1. How do these verses change the way you think about your situation in the world?

_____

_____

_____

How does Revelation 21–22 describe heaven? How does this give you hope?

_____

_____

_____

Read 1 Peter 2:9–12. When Peter describes you as God's "special" person, what are some of the implications of that?

_____

_____

Read 2 Peter 3:8–9. What are some things happening around us that could cause us to think the Lord is delaying His promise? How might this discourage us if we are not careful?

_____

_____

FAITH TESTS

1, 2, AND 3 JOHN

Everyone who goes on ahead and does not abide in the teaching of Christ, does not have God. Whoever abides in the teaching has both the Father and the Son.

2 JOHN 9 ESV

AT THE TIME OF JOHN'S WRITING, Gnosticism was sweeping through the Middle East. It was a mystical approach to spirituality, not unlike the New Age movement of our day. John responded by affirming Christianity's essential teachings, refuting false teachers, and encouraging support for faithful ministers of the gospel. In 1 John, he outlined five tests of faith that can help us expose heresies and examine our heart.

THE FAITH TEST. By saying, "Jesus Christ has come in the flesh" (1 John 4:2), John defended Christ's incarnation, humanity, eternity, and preexistence. Jesus Christ did not begin in human flesh, but He *came* in the flesh, having preexisted eternally in the Spirit. First John 5:1 affirms Christ's deity. True believers have faith that Jesus is the promised Son of God.

THE LIFE TEST. The apostle frequently contrasted what people say with what they do. And sincere believers act righteously

(1 John 2:29; 3:7, 10). While good works cannot save us, they give credibility to our confession of faith.

THE LOVE TEST. When we find ourselves able to love others the way God loves us, we confirm that we are, indeed, God's children. In John's words, the one who loves like God is "born of God and knows God" (1 John 4:7). The bond all Christians have is that they love one another the way God has loved them.

THE GROWTH TEST. God's people develop an inner conviction and ability to rise above the pressures and temptations of this world (1 John 5:4). Since the One who is in us is greater than the one in the world (1 John 4:4), we can live triumphantly! A believer's perspective reaches beyond this life, creating opportunities for growth.

THE SIN TEST. Sin does not characterize the life of Christians (1 John 5:18). This test doesn't imply that we never sin, but it does mean Christians choose obedience to God's law and authority rather than rebellion.

A VERSE TO WRITE

You are of God, little children, and have overcome them, because
He who is in you is greater than he who is in the world.

1 JOHN 4:4

_____

_____

_____

REFLECT ON THIS

How did you do on John's tests? If you failed one or more, ask the Lord for insight into that aspect of your life. If you passed all five, give God thanks for His grace at work in you.

_____

_____

_____

_____

Read 3 John verses 9–10 and 2 Peter 2:1–19. Which attributes are evident in Diotrephes?

_____

_____

_____

Why did John commend Gaius and Demetrius in 3 John?

_____

_____

_____

THE LOVE OF GOD

JUDE

~

Contend earnestly for the faith which was once for all delivered to the saints.

JUDE 3

THE WORD *APOSTASY* REFERS to people who have seemingly embraced Christianity only to fall away from the faith. An apostate is not someone who was saved and then lost their salvation. It is someone who *claimed* to be a believer but never was and then abandoned their profession. Apostasy existed in the first century, and it will continue until Christ returns.

The book of Jude is a one-page letter all about the dangers of false teachers and the temptation to fall away. Reading it can help us make the right choices when facing pressure. For those living in a culture increasingly defined by apostasy, its words offer critical insights.

Jude's original audience experienced double the pressure. They faced extreme persecution, and they were under spiritual attack from heresies of all kinds. Most of the early church's influential leaders had been martyred—including Peter, Paul, and James—leaving churches and individual Christians feeling vulnerable.

In the darkness of that moment, Jude's epistle provided a ray of hope. Verses 20–21 explain how Christians can remain committed to Christ during a time of apostasy: "But you, beloved, building yourselves up on your most holy faith . . . keep yourselves in the love of God."

Addressed to a Christian audience, the phrase "building yourselves up" conveys the idea of continuation. Jude was not speaking of a one-time event but a lifelong process. The key to withstanding apostasy is for each of us to intentionally keep taking steps that build our faith through learning, growing, seeking out God's will, and obeying everything He commands us to do.

Your walk with God is not static. You are either growing toward Him or away from Him. So examine yourself, encourage yourself, and exercise yourself in the Lord. Don't stop! Don't look back! Just keep walking with the Lord.

A VERSE TO WRITE

Keep yourselves in the love of God, looking for the mercy of our Lord Jesus Christ unto eternal life.

JUDE 21

REFLECT ON THIS

Read Matthew 7:15; 24:23–24; Acts 20:29; 2 Peter 2; and 1 John 4:1–6. What do these verses say about false prophets?

_____

_____

_____

_____

_____

Compare 2 John verses 9–11 with Jude verses 16–24. What types of people are described? Why do some verses describe a zero-tolerance policy while others commend grace?

_____

_____

_____

_____

_____

APOCALYPTIC PROPHECY

--- ❧ ---

THE REVELATION OF JESUS CHRIST

--- ❧ ---

THE WORD *APOCALYPSE* MEANS "UNVEILING," and that's precisely what the book of Revelation is. It is a prophetic book that unveils key events related to the end times. Although the apostle John originally wrote Revelation to the seven churches in Asia Minor, the book reveals details of a vision he received from Christ Jesus that are pertinent to all of God's people.

GOD WINS

REVELATION

"Now salvation, and strength, and the kingdom of our God, and the power of His Christ have come, for the accuser of our brethren, who accused them before our God day and night, has been cast down."

REVELATION 12:10

THE GOSPELS PRESENT CHRIST'S HUMILIATION— His earthly life, ministry, death, and resurrection. And the epistles give glimpses of Christ's coming glory in passages such as Philippians 2, where Paul stated that every knee will bow to Him one day. However, Revelation reverses Christ's humiliation and reveals Him as the King of kings and Lord of lords in all His glory. It anticipates the day He takes His rightful place as Ruler over all the earth. By presenting Jesus Christ in glory, Revelation places a capstone on history.

In Greek, the word for *throne* appears forty-six times in Revelation, *king* appears twenty-five times, and *power* and *authority* occur thirty-three times. When John beheld a vision of Christ's majesty, he "fell at His feet as dead" (Revelation 1:17). This response to God's glory is not uncommon, for the same thing happened to

Daniel in the Old Testament (Daniel 10:7–9). One day we too will encounter the living God, and we will find ourselves overcome by His splendor and holiness.

If you enjoy checking items off lists, get your pencil ready. Genesis portrays the commencement of heaven and earth, but Revelation depicts their consummation. Genesis describes the entrance of sin and the curse, but Revelation predicts their end. Genesis reveals the dawn of Satan and his activities, but Revelation reveals Satan's doom. In Genesis, humankind relinquished the Tree of Life; in Revelation, humankind regains the Tree of Life. Death made its entrance in Genesis, but it makes an exit in Revelation. In Genesis, sorrow begins; in Revelation, suffering is banished. All the themes that run throughout Scripture find their culmination in Revelation.

Although John originally addressed seven churches that were facing persecution, his message remains pertinent to the church of all ages. The last days are upon us. Jesus is coming, and we'd better be ready!

A VERSE TO WRITE

God will wipe away every tear from their eyes; there shall be no more death, nor sorrow, nor crying.

REVELATION 21:4

REFLECT ON THIS

What does Revelation promise to "overcomers" who identify with the Lord? See Revelation 2:7, 11, 17, 26; 3:5, 12, 21; and 21:7.

_____

_____

_____

Unlike other books in the Bible, the Holy Spirit often interprets the meaning of symbols in the text of Revelation. From the following verses, make a list of symbols with their meanings: 1:16 and 1:20; 1:13 and 1:20; 4:5; 5:6 and 5:8; 9:1 and 9:11; 12:4 and 12:9; 17:1 and 17:15; 19:8.

_____

_____

_____

_____

Revelation records seven special blessings. To whom are they given? Are you eligible to receive them? Why or why not? See Revelation 1:3; 14:13; 16:15; 19:9; 20:6; and 22:7, 14.

_____

_____

_____

NOTES

1. Henry M. Morris, *The Bible Has the Answer* (Green Forest, AR: Master Books, 2019), 17.
2. "A Bible for Every Believer," The Voice of the Martyrs, accessed July 2, 2021, https://www.persecution.com/bibles/.
3. C.S. Lewis, *The Joyful Christian* (New York: Macmillan Publishing Company, 1977), 138.
4. Hugh Ross, "Fulfilled Prophecy: Evidence for the Reliability of the Bible," Reasons to Believe, August 22, 2003, https://reasons.org/explore/publications/articles.
5. David Jeremiah, *Captured by Grace* (Nashville: Thomas Nelson 2010), 150.
6. *Sermons of the Rev. C. H. Spurgeon* (Sheldon, Blakeman, and Co.,1857), 386.
7. O. S. Hawkins, *The Bible Code* (Nashville: Thomas Nelson Books, 2020), 85.
8. Tim Keller, *The Hidden Meaning of Christmas* (NY: Penguin Random House LLC, 2016), 33.
9. This week's study was excerpted from "John: The Divinity of Christ" in The Jeremiah Bible Study Series.

BIBLE READING PLAN

The best way to see God clearly is to become acquainted with the full counsel of His written Word. This reading plan will guide you through all sixty-six books of the Bible.

JANUARY

1	Genesis 1–4	11	Genesis 36–38	21	Exodus 17–20
2	Genesis 5–8	12	Genesis 39–41	22	Exodus 21–23
3	Genesis 9–12	13	Genesis 42–43	23	Exodus 24–27
4	Genesis 13–17	14	Genesis 44–46	24	Exodus 28–30
5	Genesis 18–20	15	Genesis 47–50	25	Exodus 31–34
6	Genesis 21–23	16	Exodus 1–4	26	Exodus 35–37
7	Genesis 24–25	17	Exodus 5–7	27	Exodus 38–40
8	Genesis 26–28	18	Exodus 8–10	28	Leviticus 1–4
9	Genesis 29–31	19	Exodus 11–13	29	Leviticus 5–7
10	Genesis 32–35	20	Exodus 14–16	30	Leviticus 8–10
				31	Leviticus 11–13

FEBRUARY

1	Leviticus 14–15	11	Numbers 8–10	21	Deuteronomy 1–2
2	Leviticus 16–18	12	Numbers 11–13	22	Deuteronomy 3–4
3	Leviticus 19–21	13	Numbers 14–15	23	Deuteronomy 5–8
4	Leviticus 22–23	14	Numbers 16–18	24	Deuteronomy 9–11
5	Leviticus 24–25	15	Numbers 19–21	25	Deuteronomy 12–15
6	Leviticus 26–27	16	Numbers 22–24	26	Deuteronomy 16–19
7	Numbers 1–2	17	Numbers 25–26	27	Deuteronomy 20–22
8	Numbers 3–4	18	Numbers 27–29	28	Deuteronomy 23–25
9	Numbers 5–6	19	Numbers 30–32		
10	Numbers 7	20	Numbers 33–36		

MARCH

1	Deuteronomy 26–27	11	Joshua 21–22	21	Ruth 1–4
2	Deuteronomy 28–29	12	Joshua 23–24	22	1 Samuel 1–3
3	Deuteronomy 30–32	13	Judges 1–3	23	1 Samuel 4–7
4	Deuteronomy 33–34	14	Judges 4–5	24	1 Samuel 8–12
5	Joshua 1–4	15	Judges 6–8	25	1 Samuel 13–14
6	Joshua 5–7	16	Judges 9–10	26	1 Samuel 15–16
7	Joshua 8–10	17	Judges 11–13	27	1 Samuel 17–18
8	Joshua 11–13	18	Judges 14–16	28	1 Samuel 19–21
9	Joshua 14–17	19	Judges 17–19	29	1 Samuel 22–24
10	Joshua 18–20	20	Judges 20–21	30	1 Samuel 25–27
				31	1 Samuel 28–31

APRIL

1	2 Samuel 1–3	11	1 Kings 6–7	21	2 Kings 9–10
2	2 Samuel 4–7	12	1 Kings 8–9	22	2 Kings 11–13
3	2 Samuel 8–11	13	1 Kings 10–12	23	2 Kings 14–16
4	2 Samuel 12–13	14	1 Kings 13–15	24	2 Kings 17–18
5	2 Samuel 14–16	15	1 Kings 16–18	25	2 Kings 19–21
6	2 Samuel 17–19	16	1 Kings 19–20	26	2 Kings 22–23
7	2 Samuel 20–22	17	1 Kings 21–22	27	2 Kings 24–25
8	2 Samuel 23–24	18	2 Kings 1–3	28	1 Chronicles 1–2
9	1 Kings 1–2	19	2 Kings 4–5	29	1 Chronicles 3–4
10	1 Kings 3–5	20	2 Kings 6–8	30	1 Chronicles 5–6

MAY

1	1 Chronicles 7–9	11	2 Chronicles 12–16	21	Nehemiah 1–3
2	1 Chronicles 10–12	12	2 Chronicles 17–20	22	Nehemiah 4–7
3	1 Chronicles 13–16	13	2 Chronicles 21–24	23	Nehemiah 8–10
4	1 Chronicles 17–19	14	2 Chronicles 25–28	24	Nehemiah 11–13
5	1 Chronicles 20–23	15	2 Chronicles 29–31	25	Esther 1–5
6	1 Chronicles 24–26	16	2 Chronicles 32–34	26	Esther 6–10
7	1 Chronicles 27–29	17	2 Chronicles 35–36	27	Job 1–4
8	2 Chronicles 1–4	18	Ezra 1–4	28	Job 5–8
9	2 Chronicles 5–7	19	Ezra 5–7	29	Job 9–12
10	2 Chronicles 8–11	20	Ezra 8–10	30	Job 13–16
				31	Job 17–20

JUNE

1	Job 21–24	11	Psalms 34–37	21	Psalms 89–94
2	Job 25–30	12	Psalms 38–42	22	Psalms 95–103
3	Job 31–34	13	Psalms 43–49	23	Psalms 104–106
4	Job 35–38	14	Psalms 50–55	24	Psalms 107–111
5	Job 39–42	15	Psalms 56–61	25	Psalms 112–118
6	Psalms 1–8	16	Psalms 62–68	26	Psalm 119
7	Psalms 9–17	17	Psalms 69–72	27	Psalms 120–133
8	Psalms 18–21	18	Psalms 73–77	28	Psalms 134–140
9	Psalms 22–27	19	Psalms 78–80	29	Psalms 141–150
10	Psalms 28–33	20	Psalms 81–88	30	Proverbs 1–3

JULY

1	Proverbs 4–7	11	Ecclesiastes 5–8	21	Isaiah 25–28
2	Proverbs 8–11	12	Ecclesiastes 9–12	22	Isaiah 29–31
3	Proverbs 12–14	13	Song of Solomon 1–4	23	Isaiah 32–34
4	Proverbs 15–17			24	Isaiah 35–37
5	Proverbs 18–20	14	Song of Solomon 5–8	25	Isaiah 38–40
6	Proverbs 21–23	15	Isaiah 1–3	26	Isaiah 41–43
7	Proverbs 24–26	16	Isaiah 4–8	27	Isaiah 44–46
8	Proverbs 27–29	17	Isaiah 9–11	28	Isaiah 47–49
9	Proverbs 30–31	18	Isaiah 12–14	29	Isaiah 50–52
10	Ecclesiastes 1–4	19	Isaiah 15–19	30	Isaiah 53–56
		20	Isaiah 20–24	31	Isaiah 57–59

AUGUST

1	Isaiah 60–63	11	Jeremiah 25–27	21	Jeremiah 51–52
2	Isaiah 64–66	12	Jeremiah 28–30	22	Lamentations 1–2
3	Jeremiah 1–3	13	Jeremiah 31–32	23	Lamentations 3–5
4	Jeremiah 4–5	14	Jeremiah 33–36	24	Ezekiel 1–4
5	Jeremiah 6–8	15	Jeremiah 37–39	25	Ezekiel 5–8
6	Jeremiah 9–11	16	Jeremiah 40–43	26	Ezekiel 9–12
7	Jeremiah 12–14	17	Jeremiah 44–46	27	Ezekiel 13–15
8	Jeremiah 15–17	18	Jeremiah 47–48	28	Ezekiel 16–17
9	Jeremiah 18–21	19	Jeremiah 49	29	Ezekiel 18–20
10	Jeremiah 22–24	20	Jeremiah 50	30	Ezekiel 21–22
				31	Ezekiel 23–24

SEPTEMBER

1	Ezekiel 25–27	11	Daniel 4–5	21	Jonah 1–4
2	Ezekiel 28–30	12	Daniel 6–8	22	Micah 1–4
3	Ezekiel 31–32	13	Daniel 9–12	23	Micah 5–7
4	Ezekiel 33–35	14	Hosea 1–4	24	Nahum 1–3
5	Ezekiel 36–38	15	Hosea 5–9	25	Habakkuk 1–3
6	Ezekiel 39–40	16	Hosea 10–14	26	Zephaniah 1–3
7	Ezekiel 41–43	17	Joel 1–3	27	Haggai 1–2
8	Ezekiel 44–46	18	Amos 1–4	28	Zechariah 1–5
9	Ezekiel 47–48	19	Amos 5–9	29	Zechariah 6–10
10	Daniel 1–3	20	Obadiah 1	30	Zechariah 11–14

OCTOBER

1	Malachi 1–4	11	Matthew 25–26	21	Luke 1–2
2	Matthew 1–4	12	Matthew 27–28	22	Luke 3–4
3	Matthew 5–6	13	Mark 1–3	23	Luke 5–6
4	Matthew 7–9	14	Mark 4–5	24	Luke 7–8
5	Matthew 10–11	15	Mark 6–7	25	Luke 9–10
6	Matthew 12–13	16	Mark 8–9	26	Luke 11–12
7	Matthew 14–17	17	Mark 10–11	27	Luke 13–15
8	Matthew 18–20	18	Mark 12–13	28	Luke 16–18
9	Matthew 21–22	19	Mark 14	29	Luke 19–20
10	Matthew 23–24	20	Mark 15–16	30	Luke 21–22
				31	Luke 23–24

NOVEMBER

1	John 1–2	11	Acts 1–3	21	Acts 22–23
2	John 3–4	12	Acts 4–5	22	Acts 24–26
3	John 5–6	13	Acts 6–7	23	Acts 27–28
4	John 7–8	14	Acts 8–9	24	Romans 1–3
5	John 9–10	15	Acts 10–11	25	Romans 4–7
6	John 11–12	16	Acts 12–13	26	Romans 8–10
7	John 13–15	17	Acts 14–15	27	Romans 11–14
8	John 16–17	18	Acts 16–17	28	Romans 15–16
9	John 18–19	19	Acts 18–19	29	1 Corinthians 1–4
10	John 20–21	20	Acts 20–21	30	1 Corinthians 5–9

DECEMBER

1	1 Corinthians 10–13	11	Colossians 1–4	21	James 1–5
2	1 Corinthians 14–16	12	1 Thessalonians 1–5	22	1 Peter 1–5; 2 Peter 1–3
3	2 Corinthians 1–4	13	2 Thessalonians 1–3	23	1 John 1–5
4	2 Corinthians 5–9	14	1 Timothy 1–6	24	2 John 1; 3 John 1
5	2 Corinthians 10–13	15	2 Timothy 1–4	25	Luke 2:1–20; Jude 1
6	Galatians 1–3	16	Titus 1–3; Philemon 1	26	Revelation 1–4
7	Galatians 4–6	17	Hebrews 1–4	27	Revelation 5–9
8	Ephesians 1–3	18	Hebrews 5–8	28	Revelation 10–13
9	Ephesians 4–6	19	Hebrews 9–10	29	Revelation 14–17
10	Philippians 1–4	20	Hebrews 11–13	30	Revelation 18–19
				31	Revelation 20–22

ABOUT THE AUTHOR

DR. DAVID JEREMIAH is the founder of Turning Point, an international ministry committed to providing Christians with sound Bible teaching through radio and television, the internet, live events, and resource materials and books. He is the author of more than fifty books, including *Where Do We Go From Here?*, *Forward*, *The World of the End*, and *The Great Disappearance*.

Dr. Jeremiah serves as the senior pastor of Shadow Mountain Community Church in El Cajon, California. He and his wife, Donna, have four grown children and twelve grandchildren.

ISBN 978-0-7180-9261-0

With God, Nothing Is Impossible

In a world full of stress and fear, we need the Lord more than
ever. Draw near and bask in His promises of faithfulness, peace,
and goodness in *David Jeremiah Morning & Evening Devotions*.

THOMAS NELSON
Since 1798

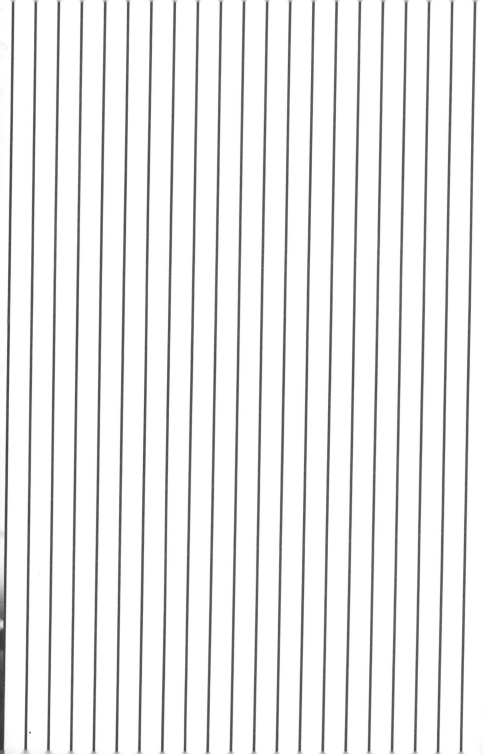